Praise from the Pros

As the veteran/victim of more than 500 how-to books, I have a favorite game: "If you were new to fundraising and could only afford three books, which titles would be absolutely worth your money and time?"

- #1 is easy: Jeff Brooks' *The Fundraiser's Guide to Irresistible Communications* (because almost every common assumption about success in this vital realm is dead wrong).

- #2 is coming soon: sometime in 2021, Jen Shang will release her definitive book on neuroscience and "identity-based fundraising" (until then *Subliminal* by Leonard Mlodinow will do nicely; or Francesco Ambrogetti's *Emotionraising*).

- #3 is this shockingly-complete new book, *Green Green* by David Love, a.k.a., *The Godfather of Good*.

I am a by-product of a thousand mentors…including David Love. I quote him often in my own training. And yet this book took me by surprise: it contains — in short chapters, charming and easily consumed (by bosses and boards) — pretty much everything you need to know about the *business* of fundraising. For instance: it replaces the crumbling "giving pyramid" model with David's eye-opening ROI-based alternative.

It is a magnum opus.

David's book might initially seem to be about "nature" causes mostly. That was the special segment of this planet's nonprofit sector where he worked long, hard and formidably. Don't be misled. David's advice, wisdom and rules of the fundraising road apply to every charity I know. Read this book. Your fundraising *will* be much more successful.

— *Tom Ahern, Tom Ahern Communications.*

When David told me he was writing a book about fundraising I was eager to read it, to experience again the clarity and conviction of *The Godfather of Good.*

Logical, highly readable and focussed, this book inspires one to action. I will purchase copies for organizations I support.

As a boss and a colleague, David was the best. He taught a fresh, not-so-sure fundraiser the Big Truth that has been *the* thread through my career: it is a privilege to work with people who want to support your cause. Be honest, creative, transparent and thorough. You owe that to them.

— *Kim Bilous, Fundraising and Voluntary Sector Consultant.*

On my first ever trip to Canada back in the 1990s, I was told, if you want to learn about legacies, donor care and the best in Canadian fundraising, go and see David Love. Thus I uncovered some of the most instructive case histories of all time and conceived huge respect and affection for the author of this book, *The Godfather of Good.* Ever since, at intervals, I've learned from this great guy and my respect and affection has grown. David tells the truth, concisely, memorably and very well.

The book in your hands is a treasure trove of rare gems. Into it David Love has poured the ripened fruits of his decades of labour in the cause of a better world and safer future for our grandkids. He recounts these here with such verve and enthusiasm it's a joy to discover them. Think of the brightest people you know who show the most promise and go buy them this book. You and they will love it and learn from it.

Thanks, David. After all these decades, you remain an authentic and unwavering voice for making the world a better place.

— *Ken Burnett, Founder and Director, White Lion Press and Founder, SOFII (The Showcase of Fundraising Innovation and Inspiration).*

A comprehensive, practical, step-by-step guide to mapping a donor journey and how to "sprinkle legacy dust" to raise money for Nature. An entertaining read from cover to cover—from a fascinating

philanthropic pedigree to a list of "Holy Sh*t Moments!". Written by the passionate, energetic and inspiring David Love, this classic book is filled with golden nuggets of wisdom for every fundraiser.
— *Gwen Chapman, Principal, DonorFocus 360.*

I've personally known and worked with David Love for 25 years and admired his work from a distance for an additional 25. In those 50 years I've not met another fundraiser bursting with greater curiosity, energy and sheer joy as David. In *Green Green*, every one of these rare traits come bursting through, powerfully and practically.

Unlike any book on fundraising I've ever read, *Green Green* delivers laughs, tears, awe and inspiration — often at the same time. Now more than ever we need fundraisers for nature whose batteries are fully charged and can learn from the wisdom, success and humility of David Love. Every fundraiser, every donor, and every young person who wants to save the planet needs to plug into this power source of knowledge, passion and proven experience.
— *Roger M. Craver, Editor-in-Chief, The Agitator.*

Despite the fact that climate change is recognized by everyone (except a few remaining dinosaur deniers) to be an existential threat to humankind, the environment sector still receives just a few pennies of every dollar we Canadians give to charities and causes.

This needs to change.

And it will change…

It will change because of my hero David Love. David is not just smart, experienced and determined as all get out. He's also endlessly enthusiastic about every single moment of his life. I have no doubt that David's enthusiasm is going to move the needle — and increase the share of our donated dollars that go to saving our planet from the very people who inhabit it.

The book in your hands is David's opus. His stone tablet. His scripture. Read this book with the reverence it warrants. Read it and absorb David's endless joy. Read it and learn. Read it and be inspired beyond your wildest expectations.

This book is David's gift to the human race, the planet — and to you. Read it and keep fighting the good fight!
— *Fraser Green, Principal and Chief Strategist, Goodworks.*

Many people regard fundraising as a necessary evil. But David Love has always practiced it as a necessary good. The result has been infectious success, in terms of value created, inspired donors and landmark accomplishments for Nature. From all of us, thank you David, for this indispensable little book and for making a real difference.

— Monte Hummel, O.C., President Emeritus and Chair Legacy Giving, WWF-Canada.

David Love has given a marvellous gift to those of us in the fundraising world! This book is chockablock with 51(!) years of wisdom, devotion, science, nuggets, history, and overall, donor love. If you haven't had the life-changing opportunity to have David as a mentor, this book is your chance! And as you know, or will read, David is an unparalleled champion of legacy giving. *Green Green* is truly an inspirational legacy for both seasoned and new fundraisers. And our donors, and planet, will feel the impact.

— Kyla Makela, VP Public Support, Birds Canada.

A must-read for any green advocate from one of Canada's most successful fundraisers. It's written with clarity, filled with history and contains much of David's unparalleled experience. This book is an inspiring journey to create value for donors to green causes.

— Burkhard Mausberg, Founder, Environmental Defence Canada and Founding CEO, Greenbelt Foundation.

Many influential high performers are described as "gurus" in their respective craft. David Love is one of the few who actually live up to that lofty characterization. He was a pioneer in the fundraising profession in Canada and has left an indelible mark on fundraising and philanthropy in this country and abroad during his 51 years in the trenches.

This book is a combination of perspiration and inspiration. On the perspiration front, it provides incredibly practical, detailed direction for the planning and execution of all manner of fundraising programs, drawn explicitly from the David's real-life experience. The inclusion of hundreds of sample check lists, plans, letters, strategic memoranda, research data, and resource lists make it an essential tool for fundraising professionals and other players in the Charitable Sector and beyond. On the inspiration front, it is replete with fascinating anecdotes and insights which illustrate the complexity of fundraising relationships, and the values and passion that the best fundraisers bring to their respective causes and their craft.

All in all, it's an insightful guidebook, energizer, and idea generator all in one.

— *Ross McGregor, Founding principal, Ketchum Canada.*

David Love shows us in masterful detail how raising money can help protect our planet. And he does it all with his renowned charm. He's one of our great fundraisers, and I'm so pleased that he has put his decades of experience into print. Everyone who reads this will become a better practitioner, and perhaps save our long-suffering earth.

— *Harvey McKinnon, President, Harvey McKinnon Associates.*

1. This book answers, once and for all, why they call him *The Godfather of Good*. There are few experts who have captured the narrative of planned giving marketing so clearly in my own two decades in the sector. David has shared all his tactical secrets in this book, so much so that it is his own legacy for the future of green philanthropy. Indeed, it is a labour of Love.

2. This book is the quintessential "labour of Love". The Godfather of Good has masterfully unpacked the love-language of green philanthropy while unpacking the hard data and practical tactical strategy using the analytical strategy of the head. God's symphony is nature, David's opus is this book that will protect it.

3. There are no passengers on spaceship Earth, only crew; The battle cry of many environmentalists. If you work with a green charity and want to truly go from passenger to active crew, this book is the road map that navigates the strategy of the analytical head, while capturing the narrative of the heart. Labour of Love? Indeed, it is his legacy.

— *Paul Nazareth, 20 year Planned Giving Educator & Expert.*

For most of my fundraising career, I have had the immense privilege and unique learning opportunities that come from knowing the incredibly energetic, inspiring and successful fundraising master, David Love. Now you can get to know him too through his wonderful book *Green Green*. Combining practical wisdom with motivation and inspiration, this book covers a broad spectrum of fundraising work in easily digestible nuggets. With tips on everything from how to get new donors to creating a legacy program, including what you should measure and how, this book is packed with everything you need to know to raise funds successfully for environmental causes. I just wish I'd had a copy during my seven years at Greenpeace.

— *Rosemary Oliver, Amnesty International.*

Halfway through *enjoying every word*, great stuff but Jesus David, I was so nervous that you had too tiny a universe for the book, but have decided not just green fund raisers will like, everyone in money raising will want to read, plus green CEOs and other collegues, foundations, government money folks, students, business school courses, libraries, international markets, and a long list of kindred spirits — and it is *valuable* information.

Most approaches for money are too earnest and boring. David Love's new money-raising book, *Green Green*, keeps it loose, up-beat, creative, and appropriately donor-centric. You will be more effective bringing in cash for your cause, if you follow his wisdom and experience.

My friends are lucky that David didn't write this book ten years ago: it would have cost them a lot more money.

At Key Publishers we always reminded ourselves: "Don't talk about your grass seed; talk about their lawn." I think anyone selling who understands the implications of this line, knows how to sell. This book puts flesh on this basic mantra.

— *Michael de Pencier, Chairman, Key Publishers Company.*

Bursting with enthusiasm and a half-century of experience, David Love's *Green Green* is the green-print to boost any fundraising goal a hundred-fold.

Love's career shows us how a relentless focus on celebrating your donor can, yes, save the world!

Love your green mission? Prepare to surf the looming tidal wave of Boomer legacy gifts arriving just in time to save the world.
— *Steven Price, President and CEO, Birds Canada.*

The word testimonial comes from the Latin word Testes which means bearing witness. The words Testament and Testicles come from the same root. Very relevant to David whose experience in Testaments/Wills is awesome. He does not write a load of balls — he is one of the wisest in the world of fundraising! It has taken him long enough to write a book but better late than never. Mind you "late" also means dead — so word choice must be careful. And wow is David is an absolute master with words and images in fundraising. He is one of my biggest heroes and is one of a few consultants who has been a fundraiser/in a non-profit marketing role for decades. This book is a lasting legacy to David and his gorgeous and very talented family (who have inherited his gift of great communication). Read it please. I love Love
— *Richard Radcliffe, Founder, Radcliffe Consulting.*

David Love is rightly called the Godfather of Good. With *Green Green*, he has written a master class on philanthropy.
— *Ann Rosenfield, Editor, Hilborn Charity eNews; Principal, Charitably Speaking.*

David Love's new book *Green Green* is many things.

First off, it's a story of his lifetime fundraising journey, chiefly for World Wildlife and other environmental groups. Every Canadian fundraiser will want to learn about the career of one of our cherished pioneers.

Next it's a fundraising primer that outlines annual giving fundamentals crucial not only to environmental organizations, but to all charities. Beginning fundraisers will learn. Veterans will find a welcome refresher.

But most importantly this is the best text book of legacy giving that I have ever read. David has largely devoted the last twenty years of his fundraising life to legacies and it shows.

So there are several good reasons to hurry out and get this book, whether you are a new or senior fundraiser or whether you are Canadian, American, British, Australian or any other practitioner around the world. Thanks David, my old colleague, for doing this wonderful book.

— *Steve Thomas, Chairman and Executive Creative Director, Stephen Thomas.*

If you are a nonprofit professional raising money for Nature this book will become your new go-to resource! Read carefully and take advantage of David's decades of wisdom."

— *Keith Thomson, CEO, The Donor Motivation Program* in Canada.*

David and I have known each other professionally for many decades. Together we share two things: a love for the Yukon, and a passion for legacies. Although the dominant theme of *Green Green* is fundraising for Nature, this book is a must-read for both seasoned and up-and-coming fundraising practitioners in *any* sector, not only the environment.

David shares countless practical tips and insights about many forms of fundraising, but at its core is legacy giving — *the* fundraising form for the coming decade. In fact, there is no other fundraising book out there like it. David has put his heart and soul into *Green Green*. It's his testament, and every reader will benefit.

— *Natasha van Bentum, CFRE (Ret.) Legacy and Outreach Advisor; Director, Give Green Canada (G2).*

David is the fundraiser who launched a thousand fundraisers. While it is easy to think that David's legacy lies with the species he has helped preserve, the donors he has inspired or the millions (billions?) of dollars he has raised to make this world a better place, those of us who are part of the David Love Fundraising Diaspora know that his legacy is also something more. It includes the infectious passion for his life's work that he has shared with colleagues through the years that showed us the real nature of the business of fundraising: inspiration.

— *Ana White, Vice President, Advancement, Toronto Film Festival.*

In the late 1980s, I decided to publish a newsletter for Canadian fundraisers, a field about which I knew almost nothing. I asked around to find out whom I should speak to about the sector. "Who are the leading experts?" I asked, and was referred to three people.

The first was Allan Arlett, the president of the Canadian Centre for Philanthropy (now Imagine Canada). The second was the slightly saintly, but devilishly effective late Dr. Ed Pearce, Director of Major Gifts at Queen's University. And the third was *The Godfather of Good*, David Love, at the time bringing in new donors by the tens of thousands at World Wildlife Funds — Canada.

Allan became a great friend and sold me a sailboat. Ed became my sector guru and presided at my wedding. And David became my direct mail marketing touchstone, fell in love with legacy marketing, and thirty years later gave me the opportunity to publish this amazing book, his swan-song for the sector he *loves*.

When I saw *Green Green* in its raw state, perfectly reflecting its author in its serious, down-to-earth, enthusiastic, rock-solid, and deceptively-simple sincerity, I thought, "A piece of cake! We'll have this edited in a couple of weeks." Only a few days later, humbled, I realized I had a delightful gem on my hands, far more complex than it appears, and packed beyond anything I had ever encountered with tips, ideas, insights, approaches, and systems, all mined from David's decades of experience in the trenches, and all bursting with the irrepressible delight he finds in his great work on the cause of Nature. What a gift!

David I mean. He embodies the best of us. He was and is a truly great gift that has enriched the cause of Nature and the Canadian fundraising sector beyond any calculation. *Green Green* is his testament, his line in the sand, and the distillation of his fundraising genius. Don't miss this chance to say, "I know him."

— *Jim Hilborn, Publisher, Charity eNews and Civil Sector Press.*

GREEN GREEN

Reflections on 51 Years of
Raising Money for Nature

DAVID LOVE

civil sector press

Library and Archives Canada Cataloguing in Publication

Title: Green green : reflections on 51 years of raising money for nature / David Love.
Names: Love, David, 1946- author.
Identifiers: Canadiana (print) 20200369385 | Canadiana (ebook) 20200369407 | ISBN 9781927375600 (softcover) | ISBN 9781927375617 (HTML)
Subjects: LCSH: Nature conservation—Finance. | LCSH: Fund raising.
Classification: LCC QH75 .L73 2020 | DDC 333.72068/1—dc23

Green Green — Reflections on 51 Years of Raising Money for Nature

Publisher: Civil Sector Press

Canada
Box 86, Station C, Toronto, Ontario, M6J 3M7 Canada
Telephone: 416.267.1287

hilborn-charityenews.ca

United States of America
2626 Glenway Ave, Cincinnati, OH 45204 USA
Telephone: 513.471.6622

Editor: Jim Hilborn
Book design and production: Cranberryink

*This book is dedicated to my miraculous family.
My beautiful wife, Ann. My glorious children Melanie,
Jennifer and Adrian. My inspiring grandchildren
Olivia, Evan, Mason and Sadie.*

*Raising money for nature drains your battery.
These precious souls filled mine for over 60 years.
And they still do.*

And to my Mum and Dad. They would be proud.

Table of Contents

List of Figures

Foreword

Dear Reader,

You're reading this book because David Love, The Godfather of Good, is a fundraising legend. And you're in for a wild ride, just as you are when you start any conversation with the energizing and electrifying David.

Today, we want to give you two perspectives that you will not find in this book, but that have deeply shaped David's character and career — and shaped this terrific book you are about to dive into.

First, David is a forever learner.

His mother used to say that he would wake up every morning as soon as he heard the birds singing, running to her bedside muttering "…*Oh boy oh boy oh boy…*" — just because it was a new day and a new opportunity for adventure. Today, that same enthusiasm takes shape as a keen and curious David constantly reviews the latest research, trends and learnings in our craft.

"Tell me more about that."

There are too many people in this world who, when confronted with new information that challenges what they have known before, respond with stunning choreography to dismiss, disprove or dissect. Not David. He leans right into it and says, "Tell me more about that." And he listens, twitching, rocking and running his fingers through his curls. His intention to remain inquisitive and curious is precious and rare. His choice to honour the lived experience and unique perspectives of others is too.

Second, David always shows up as his true self.

Always. He rarely wears shoes. He has blasted music, ranging from Gregorian chants to the Rolling Stones, in office spaces and conference centres around the world. For decades, he changed his voice mail message every day, with a reflection on the world's news, a random and quirky literary reference, or a nerdy baseball or nature fact. It was a peek into David's mind that morning, and it was always a delightful conversation spark about his passions.

By doing this — showing up to work every day as his true self — he gives you permission to do that too. In fact, he insists on it. For you. It's more common now in our sector to have language like this. Language about authenticity and vulnerability. But David has been living his truth every minute. And it's inspiring and invigorating, just like the man himself.

Through the years, David has been and continues to be a mentor of the very best kind. He listens, he advises, he calls bullshit, he supports, he cheers and he guides. His advice comes at you like a lightening bolt. And then he looks at you and gently says, "What do you think? And more important, what are you going to do about it?"

David has been an Agent of Good for his whole life and career. He reminds all of us, as thoughtful, caring, inquisitive fundraisers that being an agitator and challenging the status quo advances our sector a thousand different ways.

He truly is the soul of our work and our Agents collective.

So turn the page and with an open mind and heart, read his words and hear his voice in your head as he shares just a sprinkling of the things he's learned through the years.

…Oh boy oh boy oh boy…

Jen Love & John Lepp, Partners, Agents of Good

Acknowledgements

Throughout this book, I mention world-class fundraisers who helped, and still help me, do my job better. But I want to acknowledge two other special groups.

The first group is made up of the marvelous men and women who worked with me over 50 years creating value for nature. I can't list them here because they are legion. But to every one of them who reads this sentence, I express my deep gratitude for your inspiration, your candour, your intelligence and your constant support. As they say, if you want to go fast, go alone. If you want to go far, go together. And together, we went far!

The second group is made up of the thousands of donors who make healing nature a priority. Among blizzards of requests to help the sick, alleviate poverty, establish human rights, educate our youth, end domestic violence and much, much more, you took time to think about and do something about our embattled planet. You ROCK!

I'd also like to thank my wife Ann, daughter Jen, colleague and friend John Lepp and legacy guru Natasha van Bentum for reading early drafts of this book. They all make it better.

A final tip-of-the-hat to Kathleen McBride and Jim Hilborn. Kathleen for her crisp, reader-friendly design and Jim for suggesting I write this book and for his wise editing of it.

A Call (not to Arms) but to Hearts

Thank you for buying (or thinking about buying) this little book. In it you will discover tools to make you a better fundraiser. They come from 51 years spent raising money for *Nature*. This is my vocation — my calling — and I was called in the early 1970s when the natural world in Yukon *(see figure 1)*, grabbed me by the throat and shouted — HELP!

Green Green gathers my tools together. I hope men and women, young and old, who are considering a career in fundraising will decide to raise money to save our planet.

Wait! That's not quite correct. Raising money for *Nature* is really raising money for people…for our survival. There are of course many worthy causes in our world, but none is as important as stopping the destruction of the natural world. If we don't do this, we will become the seventh extinction.

Nature, battered and bruised, will survive and even thrive after we are gone. Whether we stay or go will be decided in the next century. If we are to stay, it will be because bright, passionate and inspired fundraisers embrace the challenge of raising money for *Nature*. People like you. And then well-funded ENGOs will slowly rebuild *Nature*.

Figure 1: In Yukon, nature grabs you by the throat.
Taken in the mountains in Kluane National Park.
Credit: David Love

And I hope this little book helps.

This book captures what I've learned about fundraising since I raised my first dollar in 1969. Appropriately, it was for Pollution Probe, one of Canada's first environmental organizations. There are plenty of great fundraising books out there, and many will be referenced in this one. But *Green Green* is different because it focuses on raising money for the environment — for *Nature*.

For over two-thirds of my career, I raised money for, and then taught about raising money for World Wildlife Fund (WWF), an international non-governmental organization founded in 1961, working in the fields of endangered species rescue, wilderness preservation, and the reduction of human impact on the environment. WWF stands for World Wide Fund for Nature internationally, but World Wildlife Fund remains its official name in Canada and the United States of America.

WWF is the world's largest conservation organization, with over five million supporters working in more than 100 countries, supporting approximately 3,000 conservation and environmental projects. Since 1995, it has invested over $1 billion in more than 12,000 conservation initiatives. It aims to "stop the degradation of the planet's natural environment and to build a future in which humans live in harmony with Nature."

I've raised money for 16 other environmental non-government organizations (ENGOs) from Birds Canada to The Wildlands League. Finally, I've served on seven boards (Bird Studies Canada, Ecojustice, Long Point Bird Observatory, Oak Ridges Moraine Foundation, The Natural Step, Nature Canada, and The Sustainability Network). Currently I sit on three boards (Birds Canada, The Nature Conservancy of Canada — Ontario Region, and Small Change Fund).

My environmental credentials run deep!

Green Green looks exclusively at the process of raising money from individual donors, which is just one — very important — area of fundraising. Huge amounts of money are raised every day from other sources, the most obvious and often the most lucrative being governments, which contribute nearly 60% of the money raised by charities in Canada. Churches, mosques and synagogues raise massive amounts for their work, and still other sources of financial support are corporations and foundations.

For some ENGOs, raising money from governments and/ or corporations is problematic. Indeed, some do not even approach these sources. But for those that do, governments and corporations can and do provide significant revenue for their conservation mission, The Nature Conservancy of Canada being one great example. However, in spite of all of the many other options, I have focused much of my career on the individual donor because it is there that the heart and soul of the mission for *Nature* lies.

A note about fundraising

The word *fundraising* will appear many times in this book. But every time you read this word; I want you to substitute "creating value." In our work with our precious donors, we do not raise money. *We create value.*

I vividly remember learning this lesson forty years ago at WWF-Canada. My fundraising (value-creating!) career was — and indeed still is — blessed with talented people who shared their secrets with me. Sonya Bata was one. An accomplished businesswoman, museum-builder, and philanthropist, she was deeply committed to the work of WWF in Canada and indeed around the world. For years, she served on the board of WWF International.

In working with Sonya, I noticed that she gave larger gifts to other charities such as universities, hospitals and big health organizations. I finally screwed up the courage to ask her why she gave so much to them and comparatively little to us. "David" she said, "you have to earn it."

It took a moment for her wisdom to sink in — what drives great fundraising is value. We create value, and *money follows value.* A more poetic way to say this is that we make donors' dreams come true. So every time you read the word "fundraising" in this book, please think "creating value."

A Note on Web References

Throughout this book, we invite readers to learn more by following web links. Most of them will be reached by going to one page on the Agents of Good Website. (www.agentsof-good.org/greengreen).

CHAPTER ONE

My Philanthropic Genetics

I was genetically programmed for a life in philanthropy. Two of my great grandfathers were knighted for their philanthropic work. My father was deeply philanthropic and paying it forward, my daughter runs a dynamic fundraising agency called Agents of Good.

Sir Joseph Flavelle

My mother's father's father Joseph Flavelle *(see figure 2),* was an earnest stock boy who went on to spearhead the building of the Toronto General Hospital. Born in 1858, he was raised in a family that emigrated from Ireland during the Potato Famine of the late 1840s and experienced economic hardship in Canada.

Joseph had remarkable business skills, and at the age of 18 became a partner in an organization selling farm products. In 1887 he left his hometown of Peterborough, Ontario with his wife Clara Ellsworth and moved to Toronto, where he was invited to become a general manager and part owner of the William Davies Company. His success at Canada's original meat packaging firm led him to become a prominent figure in finance and commerce as chairman of the Bank of Commerce, the National Trust Company, and Simpson's Ltd.

During World War I, the Canadian Government appointed Flavelle chairman of the Imperial Munitions Board. In this role he was able to correct previous mismanagement of the production of ammunition being sent overseas from Canada for use in infantry weapons. In 1917 his service was rewarded by King George V with a baronetcy, making him the last resident citizen of Canada to receive a hereditary title.

Figure 2: My maternal great-grandfather,
Sir Joseph Flavelle (1858-1939).
Photo credit: Flavelle Family Foundation

Sir Joseph devoted much of his wealth and energy to charities, needy individuals, and public service. He played an instrumental role in the affairs of the University of Toronto, the Methodist Church, the Toronto General Hospital, and the Canadian National Railroad. He died in 1939 at the age of 82.

Sir William Gage

My father's mother's father William Gage *(see figure 3),* was an athletic farm boy who built the first tuberculosis sanitarium in Canada. No one knows why he became obsessed with TB and its prevention, treatment, and cure, but he knew many families that had been devastated by the *White Plague.* In later life, he talked about a local blacksmith who was the only survivor of a family of 14.

Figure 3: My paternal great-grandfather,
Sir William Gage (1849-1921)
Credit: NSA

William became a successful businessman and the president of W. J. Gage Publishing, the creators of the famous *Dick and Jane* readers, and mounted a personal crusade to establish the first TB sanitarium in Canada. In 1894, he offered the City of Toronto $25,000 to build one, but there was no action, and at a meeting at The National Club in 1895, those present committed themselves to find a site.

Interest in the project grew rapidly and culminated in the creation of The National Sanitarium Association (NSA) in 1896 to collect and administer funds. The president was Sir Donald Smith (Lord Strathcona) and the secretary was William Gage. The newly formed association had two purposes: to build sanitaria and fund research, and it immediately began to raise money for its work.

One of the first donors was Sir William Osler who donated $25 in 1898, saying it would be his annual gift to fight TB. At the same time, Osler's wife raised money to support nurses who visited homes of people with TB — the first home service for the disease in the world.

Spurred by a $10,000 offer from the town of Gravenhurst, (which was combined with Gage's initial $25,000), the NSA built Canada's first sanitarium in Muskoka. The *Muskoka San* was the first sanatorium in Canada, the second in North America and the fourth in the world. In its early days, the sanitarium charged a fee for service, but in 1902 the Muskoka Free Hospital for Consumptives opened, the first free hospital in North America.

The NSA worked constantly to build a sanitarium in Toronto for advanced cases and for education and research, but efforts were met with opposition from local residents. Many myths persisted about TB, including that it was a disease of the poor and that it was hereditary.

In 1901, the NSA obtained an option on property near High Park, but it too was abandoned because of opposition from residents. Next, they got eight acres near Bathurst and Wychwood (just outside the city limits) but a quickly passed bylaw made it mandatory for the hospital to be 150 yards from any "habitation." Finally, a third option on property in North

Toronto was abandoned, again due to the concerns of residents. The attempt to build a sanitarium was being met with one of Canada's first cases of NIMBYism (Not in my backyard).

Fed up with the delays, for the second time Gage put his money where his mouth was, and in November 1903, he personally bought the Buttonwood Farm, 16 km northwest of the center of Toronto. On this property, the NSA established the Toronto Free Hospital for the Consumptive Poor on 40 acres beside the Humber River. As was said at the time, the site was perfect because of the purity of the air. The farmhouse on the land became the doctor's quarters, the patient's dining room and the chapel, and a wing was added to the building for beds.

The NSA handed the operation of the hospital over to a Board of Trustees, but the organizations remained closely connected until 1974 when the NSA transferred the property to the hospital. However, the association remains involved with the current West Park Health Care Centre, with two positions on the hospital board and with ownership of the property should it cease to be used as a hospital. My eldest daughter Melanie is a trustee of the NSA, making her the fifth generation to serve.

Sir William was knighted for his philanthropic efforts in 1918 and he died in 1921.

Gage Love

My father, Gage Love *(see figure 4),* was born in 1917, and eventually took over the reins of W. J. Gage Publishing from his father, Harry Love. He was an annual donor to over 30 charities, ranging from hospitals to churches to international development. In his later years, he was often asked to become a monthly donor, but he always refused, saying that he wanted to see charities earn his support every year…a lesson I learned again, many years later from Sonya Bata.

Figure 4: My father, Gage Love (1917-2005)
Credit: Steve Pugh

My dad served on the board of many charities and was a founder of The Metropolitan Toronto Community Foundation, now called the Toronto Foundation. A respected businessman, he became president of the Toronto Board of Trade, but perhaps his greatest philanthropic gift was to the environment. When Pollution Probe was established in 1969, he immediately saw the urgency of the issue, and was among the first business leaders to contribute to and raise money for the environment. In 1969 in Canada, no government agencies at any level were established solely to care for the environment, and there were certainly no senior positions in corporations that had an environmental portfolio.

My father was a philanthropic pioneer. Helping him raise money for the environment launched me on a career creating value for *Nature*.

Jennifer Love

Paying it forward, my daughter now has a career in fundraising, and she's been doing it since she left university 20 years ago. She and her partner John Lepp run Agents of Good and do some of the best value-creating in the country. I work occasionally with Jen and John and, when I do, I'm affectionately called "The Godfather of Good."

It seems that working for good is my destiny.

Figure 5: My daughter Jennifer Love, co-owner, Agents of Good
Credit: David Love

CHAPTER TWO

What Makes Fundraising for Nature Different?

Fundraisers do important, challenging work. My fundraising "hood" is the Greater Toronto Area (GTA) in Ontario, Canada, a marvellous place to do my work. There are innumerable worthy local causes for which you can raise money, but it is also one of the most difficult places to do it. That's because there are probably more fundraisers in the GTA than anywhere else in the world! The largest chapter of the Association of Fundraising Professionals (AFP) is the GTA, with more members than New York, Chicago, LA or San Francisco, a reflection of the huge number of Canadian charities that are constantly looking for money.

A central premise of this little book, however, is that raising money for Nature is different.

11 REASONS WHY FUNDRAISING FOR NATURE IS DIFFERENT

1. This issue is the most important.

I don't mean to downgrade education, big health, hospitals, international development, human rights, women's issues, and a host of other worthy causes. But without a healthy functioning Earth, all those concerns are secondary. And with climate change now putting Homo sapiens closer to the endangered species list, this has never been more true. There is no Planet B. This gives our issue unique momentum and importance.

2. We face a common misunderstanding.

Many people think that because of the extensive media attention being paid to the environment, lots of money is being donated to this crucial issue. In the mid 1980s we would have a small celebration in our tiny WWF office if our issue got *any* mention at all in mainstream media. At that time, about 3% of charitable donations went to environmental causes, but because this includes donations to humane societies, the actual investment in the environment was likely more like 1.5%. Today, despite the media frenzy, that investment has grown very little. The latest number from the Canadian Revenue Agency is 3.5% and it *still* includes humane societies.

3. We have dizzying competition

Perhaps because our issue is so important, we have dizzying competition. And not just from other, better-funded charities, but from each other. You need only look at the *Green Budget Coalition*, a group of 22 national charities working to rescue our embattled planet *(see figure 6)*.

Figure 6: The 22 organizations in the *Green Budget Coalition* 2020
Credit: David Love

That's just at the national level. Provincial and local environmental organizations are also our competitors. Folks wanting to make a gift to help the environment have a plethora of options. Part of me says this is a good thing. We can't have too many organizations engaged in the world's most important issue. But the vigorous competition from each other makes our job more of a challenge…every day.

4. Change is slow

In our business, change is slow. Victories take time, and our planet will not heal overnight. This makes our already difficult job raising money—I mean *creating value*—even harder.

5. We have opportunities to show our work in action

On the bright side, we have unique opportunities to show donors our work in action. While change takes a long time, early signs of progress can be quickly evident. This means we can take donors on great mission-based outings.

6. We are challenged to make our projects tangible

We are deeply challenged to make our projects tangible. We don't build buildings, fund schools, buy machines, release prisoners, or cure diseases. We must work hard to make it clear exactly what a donation will do.

7. New Canadians show a deep commitment to nature

New Canadians show a deep and fundamental commitment to the natural world. People coming here from other countries appreciate Nature. Perhaps this is because in Canada, you don't have to go far to have your breath taken away by it. While many charities need to work hard to create an affinity to their cause, ours flickers in everyone. It's a matter of finding out how to fuel the flame.

8. We want more than money

We share this with other charities, but for those of us raising money for Nature, it's front and centre. Of course, we want our donors' money; but we want more. We need our donors to be *advocates* for Nature. We need them to "walk the talk," to tread more lightly on the Earth. And we need them to influence others to do so — family, friends, colleagues, and elected officials. We need their money *and* their actions.

9. Fundraisers have to be environmentalists first

I think those who raise money for the environment have to be environmentalists first. Like Sisyphus, we are often pushing an enormous rock up a high hill, only to have it roll back again, and this takes an immense toll. I've seen many highly qualified folk give up on their attempts to create value for the environment. In fact, a deep commitment to the cause is a prerequisite if you want to raise money for Nature. This deep commitment to the cause will also make it easier to resist opportunities to move to a non-environmental charity. If you are good at what you do, you will be invited to leave and often for more money. DON'T!

10. Our issue can inspire us every day!

Renewed energy comes from "Vitamin N". A delicate wildflower. A bird song. A glorious dawn morning.

11. Donors are thinking deeply about the future

And finally, donors to Nature are already thinking deeply about the future. This means that inviting our donors to think about leaving a legacy gift is easier and perhaps, promises even more success.

CHAPTER THREE

Why the Focus on Individuals?

If your charity is looking for financial support, there are four major sources of revenue: governments, corporations, foundations and individual donors.

Governments at all levels contribute about 60% of all the money raised by charities, not including the money they contribute by allowing donors to reduce their taxes through tax credits. Corporations make generous donations to many causes, including the environment, and overall, provide about 7% of the money charities receive. And delivering about another 7% of the money charities receive, are the foundations, many of them specialized and focused with their support. In fact, there is even a group of foundations especially interested in supporting environmental causes, Environment Funders Canada.

There are special skills needed to successfully raise money from government, corporations and foundations, but this book will focus on the fourth and final source; those amazing individual donors who account for the remaining 26%, a huge chunk that makes all the difference. This includes people who buy memberships and other items, attend events and make donations to support the work a charity does. This book is about raising money from (creating value for) these precious people.

I chose to write about this source firstly because it is the source I know best, and from up close. Also, I feel a special need to pay tribute to those marvelous people who make donations, large and small, to make our world a better place. They aren't obliged to do this, but they do. And it is that honest expression of the philanthropic spirit in us all — as with the *Ice Bucket Challenge* and The Humbolt *Go Fund Me* Campaign — that sometimes takes my breath away.

And finally, I've been moved by the recent revolution in the way we think about and address individual donors. My early awareness of the beginning of this change came in 1995, when I read *Relationship Fundraising* a book by Ken Burnett that made the extraordinary claim (at the time) that when you raise money for your charity, the most important thing isn't the charity: rather it's the donor. This explosive idea challenged me to learn, understand and accept that the most important thing to my donors was not World Wildlife Fund. I had to rethink everything we did to raise money for Nature.

Of course, our donors want to help us accomplish our mission: that is and will always be paramount. But to maximize the money I could raise, I had to make one small but crucial adjustment in my communications with my donors. The emphasis had to change from what we do to what my donor makes possible.

TWELVE PRINCIPLES OF DONOR LOVE

This understanding is at the heart of all great fundraising, and we capture it by talking about *Donor Love*. With my fellow *Agents of Good* and other comrades in arms, we have developed twelve principles of *Donor Love*.

Figure 7: Donor Love Logo
Credit: Agents of Good

1. Do your homework

Almost every day, there is new research about how to be a better fundraiser. For instance, did you know that you will raise more money if your title is right? Or that using the word "bequest" *reduces* the likelihood you will get a gift in your donor's Will? You owe it to your donors to know about and apply the most recent research.

2. Measure what matters

If you measure things that don't help you do your job better, stop now. There's plenty to measure that does make a difference, and you'll find whole sections about measurement in this book.

3. Earn respect, invite consent, and inspire conversations

Your donors are like you: passionate and dedicated. Treat them well (if you don't someone else will!), and remember that a gift from them to your mission is not a transaction or a securement; it's an expression of their hope for a better world. Find out more about them. Get them to talk to you. The best fundraisers are active listeners.

4. Be thoughtful

Your communications with your donors and prospects should sparkle with intelligence. They are clever people; treat them as such.

5. Be accountable

Donors want to know how you spend their money to accomplish your shared mission. Provide details. Talk about value.

6. Be trustworthy

Trust is an act of faith. Let your donors know that your organization is up to the task. They have a right to know this and shouldn't have to ask. Use third-party testimonials to establish your organization's credibility.

7. Build confidence

Confidence comes from showing that you get the job done for Nature. Talk about your successes.

8. Show them they are heroes

Remember our *Donor Love* mantra above. It's not about what you do; it's about what they make possible. Your donors are heroes for Nature. Tell them that often; make them feel special.

9. Tell and invite amazing stories

Great stories are at the heart of passionate fundraising. Make your important work come alive through tales of success from the field. Your donors have stories too. Ask them to share their adventures in and for Nature.

10. Connect to your donors' values and emotions

Your donors travel on this journey with you because what you do speaks to their deepest values and emotions. Be upfront about those feelings and motivations. It will bring your communications to life.

11. Get them to fall (and stay) in love with your charity

Your donors are not bank machines from which you withdraw cash. They are caring people who want to make their world a better place, and they support your work to do this. Appreciate them, challenge them, and nurture them. Get them to fall in love with your work, and feed that love every time you talk with them.

12. Do all the small things all the time

Great thank you letters. Crisp efficiency. A warm, friendly greeting on the phone. Every once in a while, a delightful surprise. Doing the little things right will make you different from all the others. It will make your charity the one they fall in love with.

Some things in fundraising will never change…like the importance of affinity, capacity, and connection. These three things will always guide great major gift fundraising, but we are still learning about *Donor Love*. For me, raising money from individuals has always been both challenging and rewarding. And now, whole new avenues are opening up based on the simple but profound premises of *Donor Love*.

When I began my fundraising career, I was obsessed by "the donor pyramid". Most discussions of fundraising started with the pyramid because it was seen as a convenient way to look at all the fundraising activities undertaken by an organization. Specifically, the pyramid challenged us to be strategic about developing relationships with our donors; our task was to move them up the pyramid. But over the years, and especially in the light of the concept of *Donor Love*, the pyramid to me seemed deeply flawed because it focusses on the organization, rather than the donor *(see figure 8)*.

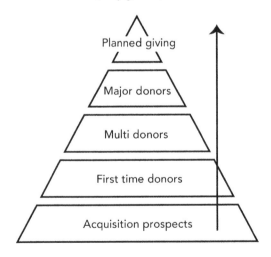

Figure 8: The fundraising pyramid
Credit: David Love

A much better metaphor, which puts the donor in the centre of the discussion, is a *donor journey*. So, in considering fundraising from individuals, we are now going to look at the donor journey. We will look at how the journey starts; we will look at the available stops along the way; and we will conclude by looking at how the journey ends.

With that introduction, let's look at how the trip begins.

CHAPTER FOUR

The Journey Begins: Build a Supporter Base

In December 1978 Monte Hummel asked me to visit him at Innis College where he was teaching. I first met him in 1969 when he, my wife Ann, and a few other zealots created Pollution Probe. I became involved as a volunteer, mostly trying to raise money for a cause no one understood or ever heard about. Monte and I worked together at Probe for three years and then went our separate ways — he to teach at the Quetico Centre and Ann and I to build and start the first independent high school in Yukon.

When we next met, Monte had just become the executive director of World Wildlife Fund Canada (WWF), an organization completely new to me. He passed me two lists of names to read. One was WWF Canada's board of directors, including names like Sonja Bata, Fredrik Eaton, Bill Harris, Dick and Beryl Ivey, William Sobey, and Maurice Strong. It was a list of some of the most successful business people in Canada. Then I read the second list, WWF Canada's Scientific Advisory Committee: Dr. Don Chant, Dr. James Anderson, Dr. Ian McTaggart Cowan, and Professor Keith Ronald. Now

I was looking at a list of Canada's preeminent biologists.

Monte said, "Don't you think that if we combine the talents of these people, we can do a lot for wildlife?" Having already been deeply inspired by the unparalleled wild beauty of Yukon, I agreed, and he asked me to join him at WWF as their education coordinator, visiting schools to talk about the magic of wild animals and majestic places.

Ten years later on Earth Day, 1988, I was in a bright room at WWF US in Washington, DC with 22 of my WWF colleagues from 14 national offices and from WWF International. We had just concluded a four-day direct mail fundraising workshop, and my head was about to explode. I had learned that, if we do it right in Canada, we can use the mail to create a base of wildlife supporters who will help us achieve our ambitious conservation mission.

We had already begun experimenting with direct mail with the help of Steve Thomas who ran one of Canada's early fundraising agencies, but I really didn't know what I was doing. After Washington, however, it became clear that I could get paid to help other people do what I wanted to do — *protect nature in Canada*.

I did not join WWF-Canada as a fundraiser. I joined as their education coordinator. But I saw that, if we really wanted to get the job done, we needed more money — lots more money. So by 1988, as the new director of membership I decided to learn as much as I could about the art and science of fundraising.

Second only to inspiration from colleagues, books were an early and constant source of ideas for me. One such enduring fundraising book is *Asking Properly* written in 1996 by George Smith, a fundraising writer from the UK. I will never forget attending a workshop George gave in Toronto about writing to raise money. He was funny, profound, thoughtful, angry, and inspiring. And so is his book. Here is a sample:

"I suggest your heart would soar if — once in a while — you received a letter written in decent English which said unexpected things in elegant ways, which moved you and stirred your emotions, which angered you or made you proud, a letter which you wanted to read from beginning to end, a letter apparently written by one individual to another individual. But you never see these letters any more."

If you write to raise money in the mail or in emails, you simply have to read *Asking Properly*. There will be other books and resources listed as you read along, but now, let's begin the journey.

Acquiring new donors

Of course, the first step is to invite people to support your cause — in my case at WWF, wildlife conservation in Canada. Acquiring new donors became our early obsession, and thirty years ago this was relatively easy. We simply traded the names of our current donors with other charities. Of course, we found that donor lists from other charities similar to our cause responded the best. And by that, I mean we might get a small donation from 3% of the people we contacted. Over time, applying this system with care, we developed a substantial and growing list of donors engaged with our mission.

Along the way, we noticed that many of the donors who gave once, did not give when asked again. Our numbers at WWF and those of my colleagues who were also building donor files were the same. Only about half of those who gave once gave again. So very early on, I learned that a donor wasn't really a donor until their second or even third gift. The key to our success would not just be getting new donors but keeping the ones we had. Donor retention became the new obsession, which continues to this day. And, in my mind at least, donor-centered fundraising was born. We needed to do all we could to make donors feel special about supporting our work. We needed to *love* our donors.

Looking back, this says a fundamental thing about the donor journey. The journey does not start with your charity. In fact, a donor joins a journey they have already begun. This explains why so many people only give once. After their first step on the journey, they often aren't really interested in continuing. If our mission fails to capture their fundamental values, they move on to a journey that does. So to acquire new donors we had to get the essence of our mission clear right from the beginning. This way, we would attract new donors who might take the next step, especially if the invitation to take that step also expressed our mission clearly.

Make no mistake. In all the talk about donor-centered fundraising and *Donor Love*, achieving the mission is paramount. Donors don't join our journey in order to be loved. They embrace our mission to save wild animals and wild places. It is our challenge to make the journey as exciting and fulfilling as possible. We do that by making our donors feel like heroes — by practicing *Donor Love*.

As a result, over time, we created a rewarding journey for our loyal donors. We fell into a pattern that worked for us and that still works to create, retain and build a strong group of supporters. The acquisition example that follows makes a few essential points about getting new donors.

One of the unique advantages to working with WWF was that we were encouraged to visit the local Ogilvy & Mather advertising agency who would help us for free! (Advertising legend David Ogilvy was on the WWF International board.) We worked with O&M and created an acquisition program that relied on people cutting out coupons from three full-page magazine ads featuring a peregrine falcon, a burrowing owl and a black rhino.

The agency created the ads and found free space for us in a range of magazines *(see figure 9)*.

Figure 9: Ogilvy & Mather peregrine falcon ad
Credit: WWF-Canada

The response to these ads was fabulous, and from 1980 through 1982, they brought in 2,300 new donors. As these donors had to take the time to fill out a coupon, address an envelope and mail it back with a cheque, they were clearly interested in the cause. They were committed WWF donors. For many years, WWF-Canada had one of the best retention rates in the country.

The lessons we learned about getting new donors from these ads were crucial to our continuing success for many years:

- The mission is front and center
- The ads have a bold intriguing headline with a clear call to action
- The ads make compelling reading; Canadians *love* wildlife.
- People who respond to these ads are likely to give again — if asked properly.

Getting new donors, however, is an expensive investment. When we invested heavily in donor acquisition at WWF, we convinced our auditors that the acquisition of new donors was a *capital*, not an *operating* expense. This allowed us to make a large investment without dramatically increasing our cost to raise a dollar on the operating side. And it also showed us the value of every single donor acquired: each one was a capital asset upon which we could draw for conservation action for years to come.

CHAPTER FIVE

The Journey Continues: Keep Track of Them

At the core of your supporter program is an accurate database where you retain information about your donors. Your database allows you to talk to every person individually, even if you have 50,000 people; but it's not just a collection of names, addresses, and numbers. It is a pulsing, impatient, passionate group of fellow travellers who want to heal the world. So regularly, instead of using the word "database", use the word "donors". Because that's what your database really is.

As we mentioned in Principle 2 of *Donor Love* on page 17, you need to measure what matters! Measure things that tell you how healthy or unhealthy your program is. Measure only things you can do something about.

Since this is a book about raising money for Nature, for the purposes of this discussion of measuring donors and money, I'll invent a charity called Climate Action Before It's Too Late (CABITL), with total annual revenues of just over $5 million and fundraising expenses of $720,000. We only need to measure two things for CABITL: donors and money. In keeping with the theme of this book, donors will come first.

Measuring donors

There is only one number you need here — Donor Lifetime Value (DLTV), which tells you how much a donor is worth to your mission. But to get this number you will need to collect some others. You will need the size of your donor's average gift, the number of times they give in a year, and the number of years they stay with you. The good news is that you can extract all of these numbers from your database — Sorry! I meant donor base.

You calculate DLTV by multiplying a donor's **average gift** times the **number of gifts per year** times the **number of years** the donor gives, and here are two examples.

If Jane's average gift to CABITL is $35, she gives 1.5 times a year and she stays with the organization for 5.3 years, her gross lifetime value is $278.25. For her net value, you subtract what you spent on Jane over the 5.3 years she stayed with you. If you spent $15 per year, your cost was $79.50. Jane's lifetime value is $198.75. If you have 2,000 donors like her, they are worth $397,500 to your mission. Now we're talking! These people truly deserve your *Donor Love*.

Of course, monthly donors deliver much greater lifetime values because they don't give 1.5 times per year; they give 12 times per year. So, if you convinced Jane to give to give $20 per month for 5.3 years, her gross lifetime value to CANBITL would be $1,272. Assuming the same annual costs to look after her, her net value now becomes $1,192.50. And 2,000 people like this are worth $2,385,000 to your mission, six times more than a regular donor! Now we're shouting! These people deserve *Donor Love* too.

The fundamental donor measurement then is net lifetime value. With this in hand, you are ready to invest intelligently in getting, keeping and growing your precious *team* of donors, the core of your program. The best book on this subject is *Retention Fundraising: The New Arts and Science of Keeping Your Donors for Life* by another fundraising legend, Roger Craver. Like Ken Burnett's *Relationship Fundraising* and George Smith's *Asking Properly*, *Retention Fundraising* is required reading if you want to understand how annual fundraising works…in other words, if you want to treat your donors properly.

In his great book, Roger talks about another important donor measure — commitment. How committed are your donors to your charity? You can find this out by asking them in a friendly survey. The committed donors with the highest lifetime value are golden. Treat them well! Or as my British fundraiser friend Stephen Pidgeon says, "Love them to death!"

Measuring money

At the end of the day, your most important overall measure is the amount of money you raise for your mission, and a robust program that raises money from individual donors (bless them!) will be involved in seven major activities. Each one of these will have a different cost to raise a dollar and a different cost-per-dollar raised.

Let's go back to CABITL and look at these two measures. The first is how much does it cost to raise one dollar *(see table 1)*.

Table 1: Cost to raise $1.00

(Total cost divided by total amount raised)

Activity	Amount raised	Cost	Net to Mission	Cost to raise $1
Acquiring new donors	$40,000	$60,000	-$20,000	$1.50 (a loss)
One-time donors	$200,000	$80,000	$120,000	$0.40
Monthly donors	$600,000	$120,000	$480,000	$0.20
Mid-level donors	$600,000	$100,000	$500,000	$0.17
Major donors	$1,500,000	$160,000	$1,340,000	$0.11
Events	$100,000	$100,000	$0.00	$1.00
Legacy donors	$2,000,000	$100,000	$1,900,000	$0.05
Total	**$5,040,000**	**$720,000**	**$4,320,000**	**$0.14**

So overall, CABITL spends fourteen cents to raise one dollar.

The second table, which is just a different way of expressing the first, is how much do you raise for every dollar spent. And overall, CABITL raises seven dollars for every one dollar spent *(see table 2)*.

Table 2: Income per dollar spent

(Total amount raised divided by total amount spent)

Activity	Amount raised	Cost	Net to Mission	Income/ $ spent	ROI
Acquiring new donors	$40,000	$60,000	-$20,000	$0.67 (a loss)	-33%
One-time donors	$200,000	$80,000	$120,000	$2.50	150%
Monthly donors	$600,000	$120,000	$480,000	$5.00	400%
Mid-level donors	$600,000	$100,000	$500,000	$6.00	500%
Major donors	$1,500,000	$160,000	$1,340,000	$9.40	836%
Events	$100,000	$100,000	$0.00	$1.00	0%
Legacy donors	$2,000,000	$100,000	$1,900,000	$20.00	1900%
	$5,040,000	$720,000	$4,320,000	$7.00	600%
Plus for administration	$150,000				
Total expense	$870,000				

Return on investment

(Net revenue divided by total cost x 100)

Your bosses, however, may want you to present the overall return on investment (ROI), and based on the numbers shown, CABITL's overall ROI above is 600%.

You may be asked about the relationship between fundraising costs and other costs, and often the fundraising costs are combined with other administration costs to give an overall figure for non-mission costs. Donors may ask, "How much of every dollar I give goes to the mission?" In the case of CABITL where administration costs are $150,000, the total fundraising and administration expenses would be $870,000, leaving a total net income for the mission of $4.32 million — 17% of the total revenue. So, for CABITL, $0.83 of every dollar goes to the mission.

I can't help but note here that if you were selling a product, let's say cars or computers or breakfast cereal, and you spent 95% of our money on sales, marketing and administration and had 5% left over as profit, our company would be considered a huge success. Yet here you are, selling not a tangible product, but a dream and you spend 17% on sales, marketing and administration and achieve an 83% profit!

You are a magician!

You will keep separate detailed tracking sheets for each of the fundraising activities mentioned above. To help out, this book includes examples of detailed tracking sheets for legacies because of their huge potential over the next 30 years (*see pages 95-99*).

Now that we have used CABITL to illustrate how to keep track of people and money, let's return to the donor journey and go back to examples.

CHAPTER SIX

The Journey Continues: Hang on to Them

The renewal mailing

Early in the year each year, we ask donors to continue their journey with us for the full year — our renewal appeal. It looks back at the things our donors made possible in the past year and looks forward to what they can help us with in our ambitious plans in the year to come. The renewal mailing allows us to talk about the fundamental values that underpin our mission.

Your renewal mailing is a pillar in your vibrant supporter base. It invites your donors to travel with you for another year. They support your mission because it aligns with their personal values, so at this point you need a deliberate plan to think carefully about the values that underpin your charity. This is where your donor's heart and your work intersect, and *brainstorming* can help you clarify those important connections.

Throughout this book, we've included suggestion for brainstorms. These are opportunities to invite folks in exciting conversations about your work and are listed in Appendix One.

Brainstorm

With colleagues from every area of your charity, take 30 minutes to think about your charity's values. To help, here is a partial list of values applicable to environmental organizations.

adaptability, altruism, awareness, balance, beauty, boldness, bravery, challenge, community, compassion, connection, conviction, courage, creation, dedication, dependability, devotion, dignity, discovery, empathy, empower, endurance, energy, enjoyment, equality, ethical, exploration, fairness, family, fearless, ferocious, fidelity, freedom, fun, giving, goodness, grace, gratitude, happiness, harmony, health, hope, independence, inspiring, integrity, joy, justice, kindness, liberty, love, loyalty, meaning, passion, peace, persistence, playfulness, power, purpose, quality, recreation, reflective, respect , responsibility , reverence, risk, safety, security, selfless, serenity, service, significance, silence, simplicity, solitude, spirit, stability, stewardship, strength, success, support, surprise, sustainability, teamwork, thankful, toughness, tranquility, trust, truth, understanding, uniqueness, unity, valour, victory, vigour, vision, vitality, wealth, wisdom and wonder.

Writing great letters

This is a good time to talk about writing letters and emails. Your program is built on great letters. We acquire donors by writing a letter to them, and we retain them by writing to them regularly. Since this has been happening for years around the world to charitable donors everywhere, we know what works and what doesn't. Essentially, your precious donors deserve letters that are inspiring, passionate, personal, relevant, urgent, and compelling. There is no excuse for writing bad letters to acquire new donors or to get additional gifts from existing donors. Here are six tips.

6 TIPS TO MAKE YOUR LETTERS OUTSTANDING AND EFFECTIVE

1. Pay attention to design.

Use large readable fonts. Make the illustrations appropriate.

2. Keep it simple.

Write at a grade 6 to 8 level.

3. Try to have a Big Idea.

Try to say something these people haven't heard before. Think about using a different voice. In *Asking Properly*, the marvellous George Smith said that every appeal should be special. Should be extraordinary.

4. Use the word "you" all the time

Count the number of times you use the word "you" and make sure there are plenty of them—and few uses of "we". Your letter is about the reader, not you.

5. Use the active voice

Always use the active voice and get rid of all participles that turn action words (verbs) into nouns which rob the words of their directness.

6. Be clear about what you are asking for

Be clear about what, precisely you are asking the reader to do. What is your offer and why is it compelling?

Of course, these tips still apply if the letter is an email.

My example of a great renewal mailing — and a great letter — is from Ontario Nature *(see figure 10).*

Mr. David Love and Mrs. Ann Love 45993853

February 26, 2020

16/7   xxT2(M)
Mr. David Love and Mrs. Ann Love

Dear Mr. and Mrs. Love,

Our 2020 vision for nature in Ontario includes **YOU**!

It's a new year, a new decade and an absolutely critical time for nature in our province. Today, I'm writing to you to share our plans and priorities for nature in 2020—and I'm asking you to consider increasing your monthly gift to Ontario Nature today.

2020 will be a crucial year of conservation action. And our *Friends of Nature* monthly donors like you are more important than ever! We're so grateful to have you standing by our side.

Nature in Ontario urgently needs you. Our leaders continue to claw back environmental protections and are not prioritizing urgent conservation and climate change action. **As a *Friend of Nature*, you are a voice for nature and you also ensure conservation action happens, in the areas that need it most.**

You and many of our members joined together in 2019 to create the Gananoque Lake Nature Reserve and expand our Lost Bay Nature Reserve! Thank you for your generous action to protect this precious place, one of the richest areas of biodiversity in Canada.

Now that this land is protected forever, we must swiftly get to work on

Please turn over...

214 King Street West, Suite 612, Toronto, ON M5H 3S6
phone: 416-444-8419 toll free: 1-800-440-2366 ontarionature.org

Figure 10: Ontario Nature 2020 renewal
Credit: Agents of Good

You can see the entire mailing here:
https://agentsofgood.org/greengreen

Thanks largely to your success in communicating your mission and your steps to move it forward in your renewal mailings, many of your donors, bless them, will choose to travel with you for many years. They will contribute to your good work regularly, either through the renewal mailing or through special mailings, which we will talk about shortly.

Those golden monthly donors

Early on at WWF, through the inspiring work of another fundraising giant, Harvey McKinnon, we learned that some donors on our shared journey were willing to become monthly donors to our cause. At the time — and still! — there were many programs that invited loyal donors to become monthly donors, and most of them talked about the benefits to the organization. At WWF, however, we talked about the benefits to wildlife and the **donor**.

Our first foray into this area at WWF was to ask our loyal donors if they would consider making a monthly gift instead of continuing with one-time gifts. I remember being floored when 10% of them agreed on our first request. In fact, if asked properly, many donors will become monthly supporters. And as shown in the discussion of lifetime value (page 30), these donors become champions for achieving your mission.

Monthly donors are so valuable that many organizations try to acquire new donors by inviting them to *begin* their donor journey as a monthly donor. We used this approach, beginning in 1995 with tremendous success through the use of Direct Response Television (DRTV). World Vision and other international development charities had been doing this for years, but no one in the environment or social justice space had tried it. We took the risk and created a one-hour DRTV program designed to recruit monthly donors. *Before It's Too Late*, hosted by Kelsey Grammar, star of a popular TV show, was so successful (we recruited 17,000 donors, 7,500 of whom were monthly) that we made another, *On the Edge of Survival*, that recruited another 13,000 donors, 5,300 of them monthly.

However, by the end of 1998 many more organizations were into DRTV, including The Nature Conservancy, Greenpeace and Amnesty International. The cost per monthly donor had continued to rise until it was no longer a worthwhile investment. We moved on but having been among the first to use this powerful tool, in just three years we had built the monthly file from 1,400 to over 14,000.

That was over twenty-five years ago, but the principles remain the same today. Monthly donors are precious. We need to acquire them with mission-based, donor-centred invitations, and we need to keep them by providing plenty of *Donor Love*.

To do this, many organizations create a *Welcome Kit* for both monthly and loyal non-monthly donors. We were among the first to do this in Canada and we even offered a *We're Listening* guarantee that was well received by our donors. WWF has stopped offering this, but it's been replaced by other communications that welcome the donor on their journey to save nature with WWF.

Welcome kits can still be a major tool in the crucial work you do to keep your donors, because retaining those you already have will raise much more money for your mission in the long run. These kits are an opportunity to be creative and to have some fun…a chance for you to distinguish yourself from your competition and, most importantly, to begin a meaningful conversation with your donors. A conversation that may lead to a legacy gift years down the line *(see figure 11)*.

Figure 11: WWF Welcome Kit
Credit: WWF-Canada

You can see the entire Welcome Kit at:
www.agentsofgood.org/greengreen

Special appeals

After you have renewed your loyal donors, or put more powerfully, after they have agreed to continue their journey with you, you have an opportunity to invite them to contribute more to achieving your mission. You do this by creating special appeals.

Many organizations do three of these a year. One in the late spring, one in the early fall and one just before year end. The purpose is to both keep in touch with your donor base and to raise more money for your mission. You invite your donors to learn more about specific aspects of your work and allow them to contribute to this work if they are so moved.

We use all the principles of great direct response here. A passionate, inspiring letter which is well-designed and easy to respond to. For an idea on how to do this well, spend time looking at great direct response appeals. I have included an example from Ontario Nature *(see figure 12)*.

Figure 12: Ontario Nature special appeal
Credit: Agents of Good

You can see the entire appeal at:
https://agentsofgood.org/greengreen

No junk mail

Junk mail is mail that's organization-centred, impersonal, dull, and predictable. Your donors and your mission deserve better. Your special appeals should be used to suggest that your donor might increase their gift. But always remember to provide a rational reason!

Unless your monthly donors have asked you not to send these appeals — a question you will surely ask them along the way — this is also an opportunity to ask them to give you a bit more. And being among your most staunch supporters, many will.

Yes: telephone calls too

In addition, for many years some organizations have used the phone for thank you calls, often using board members for these calls to great effect — a brilliant use of the phone. Universities use carefully-trained students to make these calls — with spectacular results. In fact, many organizations do this upgrade work using the phone, although in most donor surveys, the phone is ranked as the donors' least favourite means of being asked for a donation.

Nonetheless, for some donors the phone works really well. Just remember George Smith, who always stressed that on the phone we need to ask *properly*. This means using scripts that are donor-centered, listening carefully to what the donor says, and being absolutely clear about the purpose of the call.

Used properly, the phone can be a powerful fundraising tool. Specifically, many charities are now using the phone to follow up an online communication with an ask to become a monthly donor. Of course, all the essential rules apply here. How long the charity is able to keep that donor will depend on how good their *Donor Love* story is. We'll say more about this later.

Communications without an ask

You owe your precious donors regular communications designed to strengthen their bond with your mission, and two great examples are thank you letters and newsletters.

Thank you letters are often taken for granted, but shouldn't be. Every one you send should make your donor smile, including those that are automatically generated with a tax receipt or your online donations. A great reference here is *Thanks! A Guide to Donor-Centred Fundraising*, written by Penelope Burk, who continues to do valuable research on what makes donors give.

Stop reading this book right now and read all of your thank you letters. If they are dull, impersonal, and lifeless, rewrite them before you come back. It's not easy because you have to avoid all of the stock phrases and easy-to-write but empty verbiage. I promise, however, that you will feel much better when you've graciously thanked your donors. Then imagine how much better your donors will feel!

Here's a great thank you letter *(see figure 13)*.

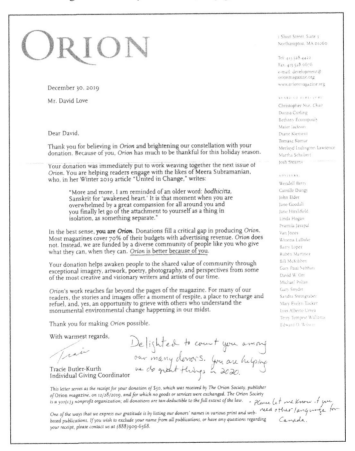

Figure 13: A great thank you letter
Credit: David Love

Donors want to see their donation in action. They want to see that they are helping to achieve your mission, which has become *their* mission. Apart from touching on these crucial things in your thank you letters, you do that by regularly reporting back to them. To repeat our *Donor Love* mantra, show them what their support makes possible, and a great way to do this is through your newsletter, packing it with powerful pictures and stories. For inspirational help with your newsletter, check out Tom Ahern's website at www.aherncom. com. Your newsletter should inform, inspire, and delight your donors, and a great example is Nature Canada's newsletter *(see figure 14).*

Figure 14: Nature Canada newsletter
Credit: Agents of Good

You can see an entire issue at:
https://agentsofgood.org/greengreen

There are many other communications you could send your donors that don't ask for money: a press clipping of a recent success; a postcard; a gratitude report; an important press release. The list of possible ways to keep in touch is endless, and of course, these communications do not all need to be printed and mailed. They can also be sent electronically, but the same writing rules always apply. Make it simple, relevant, passionate, and personal. There is no excuse not to.

Your *Donor Love* story

We used to call this the communication plan for our donors. But *Love* Story is a much more powerful and evocative phrase. In the same way that you replaced the word "fundraising" with "creating value" and the word "database" with "donors", replace the words "communication plan" with "*Donor Love* Story," the annual calendar of all the things your donor will receive. Here is the *Donor Love* Story for our imagined charity CABITL, designed for most of their regular donors. There will be additions to the *Love* story, however, for heroes (mid-level donors), champions (major donors) and legators (legacy donors), and we will look at these later in this book.

I've used the calendar year 2021 for my dates.

January 21	Renewal One
February 25	Renewal One reminder
March 9	Spring newsletter
April 12	Short thank you videos from the field
April 22	Earth Day voice broadcast thank you
May 4	Legacy invitation to selected donors
May 20	Spring special appeal
June 15	Summer event
June 24	Summer newsletter
August 17	Town Hall on hot topic

September 7   Fall special appeal
September 21   Fall newsletter
October 12   Fall event
November 30   Giving Tuesday initiative
December 8   Year-end ask or thanks

Look for serendipity

As our love story shows, a healthy program to get and keep donors is a puzzle with many pieces. Running it takes careful planning and an unflinching attention to detail, but a great program also leaves room for serendipity and flexibility, room and the freedom to follow your instincts. We learned this lesson on one occasion that dramatically impacted WWF-Canada's programs to get new donors and then to keep them.

In the late 1980s, the destruction of the tropical rainforests became a global concern. *Time Magazine* even put the issue on its front cover, and it seemed to us that we could offer Canadians from coast to coast an opportunity to do something about it. After all, many of our Canadian birds relied on habitat in the tropics for their winter home. We already had a rigorous international conservation program including work in Costa Rica, and through an arrangement with folks down there, we were able to offer our donors (and indeed all Canadians) a chance to actually buy an acre of rainforest in the Monteverde region for just $25.

Ogilvy & Mather created an award-winning magazine ad for *EQUINOX* magazine, similar to the ads we had used to find our first donors, and the response was stunning (*see figure 15 and page 27*).

Figure 15: Ogilvy & Mather rainforest ad
Credit: WWF-Canada

We were invited to appear on TV and radio to talk about the program and we even made it on to one of the most popular radio programs in Canada — *This County in the Morning*, with its legendary host Peter Gzowski.

We recruited thousands of new donors and created a special Guardians of the Rainforest program. At its core was a superb twelve-page direct mail piece that was sent each year to donors — all of whom expected it. People protected acres by buying acres for other people and for themselves. We had premiums for donors who protected 20 acres ($500 — a small silver pin) and 40 acres ($1,000 — a small gold pin).

This program added over 10,000 people to our donor base and engaged our existing donors like no other. It was all unplanned. Pure serendipity. An opportunity arose and we seized it.

Events

Millions of dollars are raised through events by many charities. The most important thing to get absolutely straight, however, is "what is the event *for*?" Among typical objectives are to raise money, to increase public awareness, and to say "thank you." Over the years, I have used events to achieve all of these goals.

In the fall of 1982, WWF-Canada held a black-tie wildlife art auction for 350 friends of WWF at the King Edward Hotel in downtown Toronto. It involved a visit from our International President, HRH The Duke of Edinburgh, the donation of work by over 100 wildlife artists, and the launch of a $750,000 program to conserve Arctic whales. It took almost one year to plan and one staff person for six months to execute this event. Wherever possible, we worked to get as much donated as possible. Our goal was to make a net "profit" of over $200,000 and we exceeded this goal. The purpose of this event was to raise money. And it did (*see figure 16*).

Monte Hummel, HRH The Duke of Edinburgh and
Mrs. Sonja Bata at November 9 Press Conference in Toronto

Figure 16: Press conference before
Spirit of the Wild Wildlife Art auction
Credit: WWF-Canada

Another important WWF event is a "thank you" occasion
for those donors who have put, or who are thinking about
putting, a gift in their Will to wildlife through WWF-Canada.
A leisurely nature walk with lunch to see the bird-banding
station at Tommy Thompson Park in Toronto. There's no ask;
just a walk. We never have trouble filling this little event, and
many people are delighted to be invited. Free for participants,
it costs very little and brings WWF-Canada's work even closer
to a very special group of donors (*see figure 17*).

Dear _____,

Every season is beautiful in a unique way, and fall is no exception. The summer sun cools, and the autumn breeze rattles the red and gold leaves above us. As this striking season ushers in the winter, there is one species that keeps busy – birds. When the crisp autumn air settles in, native birds are busy preparing for the cold, while migrant birds get ready for their journey south.

Please join WWF-Canada for a Nature Walk through Tommy Thompson Park. This beautiful man-made peninsula extends 5 km into Lake Ontario, and is recognized as a globally significant bird area. Here, we will learn about the protection of birds and their habitats through the monitoring and research done at the Bird Research Station. Then, we will trek through the Cell One wetlands to see how a confined disposal facility can be transformed into a functional, biodiverse habitat.

Join us for a journey through Tommy Thompson Park.

Wednesday, October 5, 2016

10:00 am – 1:00pm

Tommy Thompson Park

1 Leslie St, Toronto, ON

Light lunch will be provided

Please wear comfortable walking attire

The Golden-Crowned Kinglet, one of the most commonly banded birds in the fall, will be getting ready to fly as far south as Texas!

Space is limited. Please contact Sarah Zachariah at 416-489-4567 ext. **7311** or by email at szachariah@wwfcanada.org by **Friday, September 30, 2016.**

For a living planet,

Monte Hummel, O.C.
President Emeritus & Chair, Legacy Giving
WWF-Canada

Figure 17: Invitation to a special legacy event
Credit: WWF-Canada

Carefully planned events can add energy and inspiration to your annual program. Of course, they can also be used to attract new donors, an increasingly challenging area of fundraising. But whatever the objective, you always need to think through exactly how you will turn an event participant into a loyal donor…and you need to track your results rigorously.

CHAPTER SEVEN

The Journey Continues: Forge a Team

As organizations grow, they become complicated, and as fundraisers we need to understand the important roles other teams play in our shared goal to accomplish our mission. For WWF-Canada, this happened at the end of the rainforest campaign described earlier.

In 1978, we had 1,200 donors, revenue of $210,000 and three staff. After the campaign in 1994, we had 50,000 donors (3,000 monthly), revenue of $7.4 million, and 31 staff in four teams — Conservation, Communications and Education, Fundraising and Finance, and Administration.

Of course, having an enlightened boss is important. See Appendix Two (page 122) for the seven traits of a great boss.

To make sense of our increasingly complex organization, I created a *Rocket Ship* analogy.

The Rocket Ship: where are we going?

At the core of any organization is the mission. Your mission is a statement of ultimate purpose. For our rocket ship, the mission is the *destination of the ship* — the most important piece in our analogy. Currently, for example, WWF best expresses its mission in this short message that leaves no question as to whether WWF knows where it's going:

> **Why are we here?**
> *We are creating solutions to the most serious conservation challenges facing our planet, helping people and nature thrive.*

Once the destination is clear, it's time to build the ship. It has three parts: Program, Marketing, and Operations.

How will we get there?

The **Program** is the *front of the ship* where the crew determines how the rocket will get to its destination. How will we accomplish our mission? Which projects should WWF undertake? How do we evaluate them? How do we rank them? What resources will they take? Remember, the value of your organization will always be seen through the programs it undertakes.

The fuel for the journey

Marketing provides *the fuel* for the rocket's flight: financial resources, skills, time, people's networks, other non-financial resources, etc. Once the Program people determine how to achieve the goals and what it will take to do so, the Marketing people go into action.

Bringing it all together

The third part of our ship is **Operations,** a crucial element that ensures that marketing, program, and mission work well together. In our rocket ship, Operations is the *O-Ring,* the mechanism that ensures the fuel gets to the front of the ship as effectively and as efficiently as possible. Usually, Operations looks after four things: finances and budgeting, overall administration, information technology, and most important, human resources. Our rocket ship analogy confirms the importance of all three parts of the ship, and the failure of any one of them — Program, Marketing, or Operations — dooms the mission.

Much of Marketing is fundraising, but it also includes communications. This little book is about fundraising from individuals, but communications play an important role by building profile and catalyzing influence. In the process, a well thought out communications program serves at least two audiences; external and internal.

Communications folk work hard to convince the outside world that your organization is truly *important*. Among their external audiences are government officials, corporate leaders, journalists, and a host of others who need convincing. But they also talk to internal audiences, and most important for your fundraising, your existing and potential donors. It is crucial that the tone of these communications complement, support and reinforce your fundraising messages. Your ideal mantra: "It's not about what my organization does; it's about what my donors make possible."

For external audiences, the communications message must often be about what the organization does, but your communications folk need to be reminded that donors are different and deserve a more inclusive message. They don't need to hear over and over about how great the organization is. They already know that! They need rather to be hearing about the ways in which you are earning that reputation, and how their support is helping make it all happen.

In a nutshell, this means that *organizations need to ensure that fundraisers control the message to donors.* The easiest way to ensure this is to establish communications as part of the marketing side of the rocket ship. Of course, communications plays a role in sharpening and describing the program, but in the end, its role is to generate fuel to achieve the mission.

CHAPTER EIGHT

The Journey Continues: Hunt for Major Gifts

After the success of the Guardians of the Rainforest campaign, WWF suddenly had a large number of new donors and a significant number of donors who were giving $500, $1,000, and more every year. Both were new experiences for us.

At the time, another one of my mentors was Richard Hamilton, in charge of fundraising for WWF International. A well-respected fundraiser who had done marvellous work for many charities in the UK, his role was to help other WWF offices fundraise more effectively for Nature. In Canada, he patiently helped us through the labyrinth of direct mail acquisition and the complexities of a direct mail annual program. One day I said to Richard that direct mail seemed expensive and, frankly, not that profitable. He looked at me and said, "Oh for heaven's sake David! You spend all this time and money on building a large, loyal donor base for two reasons. Some of them will make major gifts, and some of them will leave a gift in their Will to WWF. And let me assure you, you will find these things immensely profitable. If you don't have strategic major gift and legacy programs, you shouldn't build a donor base at all!"

So we entered the next phase: the world of major gift fundraising. It was clear that involved two activities — a leadership giving program and personal major gift solicitation. One of the basics of fundraising is that to get the most from your donors, you need to ignite their affinity, determine their capacity and establish a connection. Affinity — Capacity — Connection. Major gifts are mostly concerned with the last two — capacity and connection. And legacy gifts are about affinity.

The beginning: leadership gifts

Richard liked to use the metaphor of a pond for our loyal donors. He asked me to think about our donors as fish in a pond into which we would cast some bait. Sometimes, fish took the bait; sometimes they didn't. But several fish took more and more bait and they became bigger and bigger. We took great care to understand the size of our fish! Through their donations, your donors let you know their capacity. You already know their affinity; they are, after all, loyal, regular, and monthly donors.

Your donor software can easily produce the numbers you need. They are called value bands and I recommend tracking seven bands.

$1 - $49
$50 - $99
$100 - $249
$250 - $499
$500 - $999
$1,000 - $2,499
$2,500 - $4,999

Of course, you will also track those who give at a higher level — $5,000+. $10,000+, $20,000+, and so on. Without question, you will treat *these* people on an individual basis.

Step One in your strategic major gift program is to identify and work with your leadership donors, and you'll need to determine the appropriate level, which, depending on a number of factors, will be different for every organization. Many small organizations start with donors who give $250 or more in a year. Larger organizations can set the major gift portal at $5,000 per year. Or higher.

Like the annual program, the lifeblood of your leadership program is compelling, relevant, inspiring, passionate, and increasingly personal appeals. A truly great leadership donor campaign is simply a high-level direct mail campaign — or online campaign, if that's what your donors seem to prefer. An example of a great leadership mailing is one produced by The Nature Conservancy of Canada *(see figure 18).*

Figure 18: Invitation letter to join Leaders in Conservation
Credit: The Nature Conservancy of Canada

SIX RULES FOR A CASE FOR SUPPORT

Leadership donor mailings often follow the standard rules for a good **Case for Support**. An effective and powerful case needs to answer six key questions:

1. What is the opportunity?
Often, this is a simple statement of the problem, outlining the fundamental issue that you want to address.

2. What are the possibilities?
Donors are looking for solutions, not problems. What is possible? What are you proposing to do to seize the opportunity or confront the problem?

3. Why Now?
Time is precious and many issues ignite a donor's passion. Why do we need to take action now? Urgency often drives response.

4. Why You?
Why is your organization the one to tackle this issue? Talk about past successes.

5. Why Me?
In our donor-centered world, this is perhaps the most important question. It needs an honest, compelling and genuine answer.

6. How Can I Help?
The answer is usually by giving money. But is there something else the donor can do to deepen their engagement with the issue? Can they recruit their friends?

Your goal is to move your precious donors through the bands — to allow them to show you their capacity. At the $1,000 level, you might start a club to make folks feel a little more special. Of course, there will always be some benefits to joining this club. Again, The Nature Conservancy of Canada has done this well (*see figure 19*).

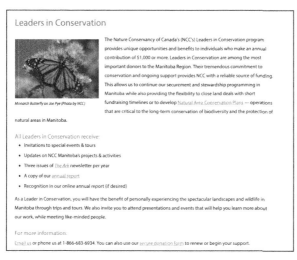

Figure 19: Leaders in Conservation benefits
Credit: The Nature Conservancy of Canada

There is a goldmine in leadership donor programs. My friends at Goodworks call these marvellous people *Hidden Heroes*, an excellent label for the people who can and will drive your mission forward. By focusing on this group you will not only raise more money, but you will also be developing your major donors, the people who can help you transform your organization's potential when you begin to approach them personally.

The payoff — individual asks

Every organization will decide at what level a donor requires individual attention. Of course, great direct response infused with *Donor Love* makes *all* donors feel special. But some donors, those who show both deep affinity and great capacity, deserve personal attention. And we all know that when it comes to fundraising — creating value — nothing beats face-to-face.

In the major gift business, we need to dream big, take risks, and demonstrate that a major gift will lead to fundamental change. Over the years, I developed my *Eight Rights Formula* (*see box on next page*) for major gift fundraising. Let this guide your thinking about getting major gifts. If you can, before a major ask, a role play with a co-worker can be very helpful. Think of the possible barriers to a "yes." In the midst of an ask for $1 million, you don't want to be blindsided by a question from left field you've never previously considered.

Along with my *Eight Rights*, be aware that in the major gift world, you must, as they say in the movie *Glengarry Glen Ross*, Always Be Closing, the **ABC rule**. Major gifts are about big money for your cause. When the cultivation process is over, you must make the ask and move on. At the end of the day in the major gift world, you must close the gift.

Finally, never forget that every major gift is really all about the next major gift. Your major donors are on a journey with you to help accomplish your mission. Once you get a major gift, start thinking about the next one. And you do that through spectacular donor stewardship — *Donor Love*.

EIGHT RIGHTS FORMULA FOR MAJOR GIFTS

1. After the right research
This research answers the seven other following "rights." When answering them, be creative. It is unlikely yours is the only organization asking this donor for a major gift. Your Ask needs to stand out. It needs to be outstanding!

2. The right person
Who should make the Ask? Sometimes it's the CEO. Sometimes a volunteer. A fundraiser. Or perhaps a client of your services.

3. Asks the right prospect
This is where typical donor research comes in. The more you know about the donor and their priorities, the more likely you will get a "yes".

4. For the right project
Know enough about your donor to take them the *right* project…for them. Those six key **case for support** questions (page 62) need to be answered for a personal major gift Ask as well. The project needs to shine.

5. At the right time
Over lunch? At an event? First thing in the morning? Give it some thought.

6. In the right way
The answer will almost always be "in person." Perhaps with a brief outline of the case followed by a direct Ask made by the right person!

7. In the right place
In an office? At an event? In the woods?

8. For the right amount
Once again, traditional donor research will help here. Remember to be ambitious but realistic!

The magic of a capital campaign

With the big charities — hospitals, universities big arts, big health — the ultimate test of a major donor program is a successful capital campaign. At its core, it is intended to get your current major donors to give more and to attract some new donors who have been waiting for you to broaden your fundraising horizons and *think big*.

The success of a capital campaign relies on a well-developed pipeline or more appropriately *lifeline* of donors who have been with you for at least three or four years. A campaign allows you to ask your special donors to step up for a short time (three to five years) and make an extraordinary gift to achieve an extraordinary result.

That result is often a new building or machine or some other capital asset, but most environmental organizations neither need nor intend to build anything. *We need/want an unprecedented investment in Nature conservation!* Nonetheless, this has not deterred organizations that buy land from running highly successful capital campaigns. As I was writing, The Nature Conservancy of Canada completed a $750 million campaign, and several other land trusts are running campaigns of between $10 and $15 million.

But back in the early days of WWF, the key question was "Could we use all the advantages of a capital campaign to simply raise more money for Nature?" We thought so and in 1995, once again went to the experts, this time Ketchum Canada, the country's largest capital campaign consultancy. The chairman, another personal mentor, Ross McGregor, was keenly interested to see if we could pull it off.

Called *The Nature of Tomorrow*, it was one of Ketchum Canada's first *programmatic* capital campaigns. With their help, we developed the materials (including our first-ever feasibility study), set the target at $10 million and the timeline at five years, and identified the prospects. To everyone's delight (and to some surprise) we reached our goal! Most of this money came from long-time personal and corporate donors, many of whom had personal relationships with Monte, other staff at WWF, and of course the conservation mission of WWF (*see figure 20*).

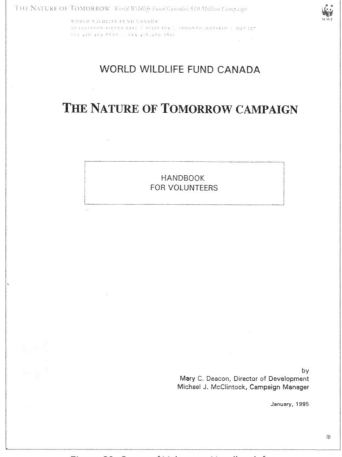

THE NATURE OF TOMORROW *World Wildlife Fund Canada's $10 Million Campaign*

WORLD WILDLIFE FUND CANADA
90 EGLINTON AVENUE EAST | SUITE 504 | TORONTO, ONTARIO | M4P 2Z7
TEL 416.489.8800 | FAX 416.489.3611

WORLD WILDLIFE FUND CANADA

THE NATURE OF TOMORROW CAMPAIGN

HANDBOOK
FOR VOLUNTEERS

by
Mary C. Deacon, Director of Development
Michael J. McClintock, Campaign Manager

January, 1995

Figure 20: Cover of Volunteer Handbook for
Nature of Tomorrow campaign
Credit: WWF-Canada

Well-planned mid-level and major gift programs, carefully and consistently executed, will take your fundraising to the next level. And they will raise exponentially more money for your mission.

CHAPTER NINE

Why Mount a Legacy Gift Program? The Case for Support

Legacies are the biggest and most rapidly changing fundraising source and hence, this is the most important part of my book. In many ways, I wrote the rest of the book to set up the opportunity to talk about the magic of legacy gifts.

Earlier I mentioned Richard Hamilton, who pointed out that the only reason we go through the expense and hard work of building a strong supporter file is because, if we do, some wonderful people will make major gifts — perhaps only 5% of them — but that 5% will make large gifts to help you achieve your mission! As you read in the previous chapter, there is a goldmine in cultivating and closing leadership and major gifts.

However, it was not major gifts that truly caught my interest. It was that these people might also make a legacy gift — a gift to wildlife in their Will or through another option in their estate plan. And remarkably, many more people are likely to leave a legacy gift than make a major gift. Certainly, major donors are an excellent target audience, but Richard also told me that legacy gifts would also come from our regular donors.

Four types of legacy donors

First let's review the kinds of legacy donors you will find. There is more detail about these groups on page 81-87, and you may well break them down further into sub-categories, but for now, there are four kinds of legacy donors on which to focus.

The Departed

The departed are those who have passed on and left your charity a gift in their Will or estate plan.

Pledgers

Pledgers are those who have told you that they have put your charity in their Will or estate plan. Some organizations refer to these people as intenders or expectancies.

Prospects

Prospects are those who have told you in one way or another that they are thinking about or will think about putting your charity in their Will or estate plan.

Suspects

Suspects are people in your donor file — or potentially not donors — whom *you think* would consider putting your charity in their Will or estate plan.

To be as specific as possible, most of the examples I use will be from WWF-Canada. I helped launch their legacy program in 1982 and worked on it full-time for 17 years until 1999. I then consulted on and off with the program between 2000 and 2014; and then in 2015, filled a maternity leave and worked on it three days a week until 2018.

I still stay in touch with WWF. It's not a perfect legacy program but it is respected nationwide as a highly successful strategic program. When I left in December 2018, WWF's *Legacy Lifeline* had 1,845 pledgers, 1,500 prospects and 2,234 suspects, for a total of 5,579 precious people. In 1982, we had no one.

You are likely familiar with the term "donor pipeline," an apt metaphor to help keep track of the current status of your major donor program. For legacies, and for environmental reasons, however, I prefer the term *Legacy Lifeline*. It allows you to treat those lovely people with a bit more love. Their legacy gift is about their life!

This chapter takes a closer look at cultivating those legacy gifts. We'll begin with why now is the time to invest heavily in legacy gifts and why senior staff in your organization will embrace this investment. Taken together, this is a mini case for support for a legacy program.

Why the time is right for a legacy program

In fact, those legacy gifts represent a powerful potential long-term lifeline for your organization. There will never be (nor has there ever been) a better time to invest in legacies, and a range of factors are driving this unique, *time-limited* opportunity.

First of all, our world is ailing in so many ways, and crying out for change. As the COVID-19 pandemic last year showed us, we are facing serious, complex issues and to address them we'll need an exponential growth in money invested in change. We need to stop the destruction of nature, address the threat of climate change, and tackle global poverty and hunger. We need to find cures for killer diseases and put an end to child abuse and domestic violence. And so much more. Our embattled planet cries out for change. Not next year. Now.

Also, the baby boomers are coming, and they will leave legacies. These are folks born between 1946 and 1965, the years Environics uses for their work and the years Michael Adams used for his wonderful book about boomers, *Stayin Alive*. You can read more about his work on page 128. While they have managed to control their world for the most part, the boomers will not avoid death! And many will leave a legacy gift before they go. Research done in Canada by Fraser Green at Goodworks shows us that boomers are *almost* as likely to leave a legacy gift as the civic generation (born before 1946), 12% of whom say they will leave a legacy gift. While only 11% of boomers say they will, since they outnumber civics by 2/1, boomers accounted for one-half of the charitable bequests in Canada in 2014 (*State of the Legacy Nation 2014* from Goodworks).

$6 trillion on the move

Boomers will inherit huge amounts of money, the most recent estimate was that in the next 30 years, $6 trillion dollars — also known as six million million! — will be transferred from one generation to the next in Canada. Meanwhile, the Boomers are convinced they can change the world. For their working lives, they may have pushed their hopes and dreams for a better world to one side, but they will likely rediscover it in retirement!

We can talk with these folks in so many different ways. We can write a long, thoughtful letters, survey them online, or inspire them with a short video. We can call or text them on their phone or delight them with an unexpected "thank you." Boomers are available everywhere, all the time, and they're delighted to hear from us if we talk to them properly. And while they won't avoid death, boomers love the idea of living forever through a significant legacy gift to an organization that expresses their hopes and dreams for the world.

Another important factor making legacy gifts happen now is the significant growth in childless couples and in people living alone. Research confirms that these two groups are ripe for a legacy gift. Without a life-partner or a child (and even more significantly, a grandchild), these folks long to *leave their mark* on the planet.

The demographic argument is perhaps the most compelling. In 2017, there were 600 million people in the world over 65. In 2050, that number will be 1.5 billion people! The audience for legacy gifts will more than double!

All of the well-funded and established charities such as Sick Children's Hospital in Toronto, the National Arts Centre, Canadian Cancer Society, and all of the universities are investing fortunes in legacy fundraising. Without question, there's a carefully calculated financial reason for this focus, and you may assume that they are *already* calling your donors about legacy gifts. Smaller charities, with their own deserving Mission to support, can learn and steal ideas from these charity giants.

Finally, research is being done on all aspects of legacy giving. Almost every month this research provides new insights on ways to obtain legacy gifts and on the motivations for legacy gifts. This all creates a unique opportunity for legacies.

Why you should invest in a legacy program

There are many reasons why your organization should embrace this explosive opportunity, and here are only six of the most significant. To make it more relevant, I will talk about the *why* from the point of view of your senior staff.

1. Legacy gifts are important for *your president or executive director* because legacy gifts advance the mission and are largely unrestricted. The precious donors who leave a legacy gift do so because they are committed

to your mission, and their gift is rooted in their desire to see your mission accomplished.

2. Legacy gifts are important for *your finance leader* because they produce a spectacular return on investment (ROI). Even the very best fundraising activities operate at a ROI of 100%. (It costs $500 to raise $1,000). Typically, legacy programs will have an ROI of over 500% (It costs $167 to raise $1,000).

3. Legacy gifts are important for *your program leader* because legacy gifts bring in *big money* for projects. The average size of legacy gifts varies widely, but can be quite large, and is always significant. In Canada, the average legacy gift is just under $30,000, but at WWF, it's about $75,000. Leading universities generate twice as much again and more.

4. Legacy gifts are important for *your major gifts leader* because some legacy donors will become new major gift prospects. Most often, legacy pledgers come from your membership file, and your legacy program will uncover hidden potential for major gift work.

5. Legacy gifts are important for *your membership leader* because pledgers will usually increase their annual gifts. Research shows that legacy pledgers dramatically increase their annual giving.

6. Legacy gifts are important for *your communications leader* because pledgers will share great stories. People leave legacies to be remembered. In most cases, the reason for the commitment to the mission is based on a moving personal story. These donors are often happy to share these inspiring stories, which will in turn inspire other legacy pledges.

So the opportunity is immense, and a strategic legacy program can — and will — transform your organization. But I've saved the most important question in any case for support to the end: "Why me?" Which brings us to your marvelous donors.

Your committed donors have already earned the right to leave a legacy gift — the most meaningful — and often the largest — gift they will make in their lifetime. They long to perpetuate their fundamental values and it is your obligation, indeed your privilege, to grant them this opportunity. They support you because your organization reflects their values. Through a legacy gift, their values live forever.

CHAPTER TEN

The Art and Science of Legacy Programs

It's about *why*. Not *how* or *what*.

When I began in fundraising, legacy gifts were considered to be the domain of major donors. Back then, the thinking was these gifts were mostly about tax advantages, which would, we assumed, mainly be a concern for the wealthy. But when Ken Ramsay, one of Canada's leading fundraisers, started to market legacies to a larger group of donors, he found them very receptive to considering a gift in their Will for their favourite charity. Ken demonstrated that the motivation was not primarily financial. It was deeply personal. We could attract these gifts not by talking about *how* to do it (get a Will) or *what* to do (talk to your financial advisor) but by talking about *why* the donor should consider it.

We know now that this applies to many things as well as getting legacy gifts. To see the concept described in a compelling nutshell, check out Simon Sinek's TED talk *How Great Leaders Inspire Action*. His *Golden Circle* has profound implications for fundraising *(see page 128)*. This does not mean that *what* or *how* don't matter. But they come after *why*.

Another way to look at this is that you will get the commitment for a legacy gift by appealing to your donor's emotions. Then, once committed, donors will become increasingly interested in the *how* and *what*. My friend and legacy expert Fraser Green at Goodworks calls this engaging the heart, then the head. In the last few years, I have worked with the Agents of Good to make this approach come alive. A good legacy program needs a compelling *why* brochure and a great *how* letter which talks about the why and how of legacy giving. You will find samples of both on pages 114 and 116.

It's about getting a gift in a *Will*

In the early days of legacy fundraising, we felt we needed to talk to our donors about all the options they had to include a gift in their estate plan. They could leave a gift of life insurance. They could donate registered retirement funds. They could create a charitable annuity or a charitable remainder trust. They could make a gift of residual interest and they could leave a gift in kind. And that's not all! A confusing list of technical options indeed!

The good news, however, is that even with this plethora of opportunities, well over 90% of legacy gifts are gifts in Wills — charitable bequests. Of course, you still need to know about these other options. After all, you are talking to your donor about the most significant gift they will make in their lives, and one of these other options — or a combination — might be the best way to proceed. But in setting up your program and marketing it, talk first and primarily about Wills. And if your donor gives through direct mail, they likely already have a Will, so you can move right to the central focus on the possibility of a legacy gift to your organization — why should the donor do it?

It's about learning what *works*

In 1676, Isaac Newton wrote, "If I have seen further it is by standing on the sholders (sic) of giants," and there are some legacy giants upon whose shoulders I suggest you stand. In the UK, there are Richard Radcliffe, who is a global authority, Claire Routley, Ashley Rowbottom and Adrian Sargeant. In the US there are Russell James, Michael Rosen and Greg Warner. Right here at home, we have Ken Ramsay, Penny Burke, Fraser Green, Ligia Pena and Natasha van Bentum. Of course, John Lepp and Jen Love at Agents of Good do some of the best legacy work in Canada.

In addition to these practitioners, you can find some of the best legacy fundraising done by checking out the legacy examples on the wonderful SOFII website. SOFII stands for *Showcase of Fundraising Innovation and Inspiration* and this site has some fabulous legacy examples (www.agentsofgood. org/greengreen).

It's not about death. It's about life

Often, fundraisers and volunteers say that they don't like talking about gifts in Wills because they feel they are talking about death. This, however, is a mistake. Research in the UK shows that donors who make a gift to charity live longer than those who don't. If they leave a legacy gift, they live even longer!

***

With these basic concepts under your belt, your organization needs to be structured to address the operating challenges and to do what is required to make your legacy program soar. Your first objective must be to get board and senior staff buy-in.

Your strategic legacy program needs support from the top. Find people on your board and senior staff who will be your legacy champions. Of course, this means that your champions will have agreed to make a legacy gift themselves. It is difficult for a volunteer to invite a donor to leave a legacy gift unless the "asker" has also done it.

You'll need a long-term financial commitment at senior levels of your organization. While there are fundraising programs you can abandon, such as an acquisition program that's not performing, or an event that doesn't work, you can't stop a legacy program. To do so would betray your most precious donors. Getting a legacy gift will take time, and there may be decades between when the pledge to make a gift is made and when the gift is realized.

One way to finance a sustainable program is to get senior management to agree to let you invest a percentage of unrestricted legacy gifts into building a strategic legacy program. Because these gifts are almost always unrestricted and large, you only need five percent. The fact that you are asking for a small amount of money which has not yet arrived, may make the management decision easier.

You will have to make compelling and ongoing arguments to maintain your investments in legacies. Far too often, organizations struggling with their investment in fundraising decide to cut acquisition programs and/or legacy programs. Nothing is more short-sighted...especially considering the approaching legacy tsunami (*see page 71*) that you stand to miss by simply doing nothing.

From greatest hits to fondest dreams to future vision

Brainstorm:
Create a list of your organization's *Greatest Hits*

Donors considering a legacy gift need to see clear evidence of past success. As Shakespeare wrote, "The past is prologue". Set aside time at a staff meeting to come up with your greatest hits over the past five or ten years. This exercise is a lot of fun and it will draw your staff closer to the mission. Once you have agreed on this list, find 30 minutes at your next board meeting to present the list to them. You'll really enjoy listening as the board argues about what your greatest successes were! The result will be a far cry from the usual conversations at bored—sorry—board meetings!

Brainstorm:
Follow up with a list of your organization's fondest dreams, and from that create your future vision

After confirming your success, take time to enunciate your fondest dreams. What would you like to see happen in the next 10, 20 or 30 years? Your results should be dynamic, ambitious, realistic, and exciting. Your legacy prospects and pledgers will be deeply interested in your thinking...after all, this is what they will be investing in.

You'll find some examples of future visions in Appendix Seven. While many charities struggle with a visioning process, supporters of environmental organizations rarely need to be convinced about thinking about the future. In fact, they do it all the time. But insist on rigourous clarity. What is your specific charity's future vision? How will the world be different as a result of your work in 10, 20 or 30 years?

Show legacy impact and keep track of your legacy donors

Let your donors know how legacies have advanced your mission and be as specific as possible. This is easy for many organizations for which legacy gifts have built buildings, bought machines, and established transformative programs. It is not easy, however, for us in the environment field to demonstrate impact. Think creatively about species rescued, habitats restored or purchased, and destruction slowed down. Your results will drive legacy gifts, and you need to recognize and keep track of all four types of legacy donors — the *Departed*, the *Pledgers*, the *Prospects* and the *Suspects*. The last three of these are your legacy lifeline.

Your *departed*

The departed are those wonderful folks who have left you a legacy gift, and they are in two categories. The first is closed estates — donors who have passed on and whose gift to you in their Will is complete. Your charity has received all the money you will get.

The second group is open estates where you have been notified that your charity has been named in a Will. This marks the beginning of a long process of negotiation with executors, lawyers, and ultimately the Canadian Revenue Agency (CRA).

Some of your open estates will be contingent where the donor has passed on but the Will will not be enforced until something else happens, often the death of a surviving spouse. There is not much you can do for contingent estates; just be aware of the contingencies and take any action necessary.

There are things you can do with your other open estates. I recommend a call with the lawyer or executor at the beginning and then a system of regular follow-ups until the estate is finally closed. This can take between 18 months and two years, and sometimes even longer.

There are usually at least two payments from open estates. The first is an initial payment where some but not all of the estate is distributed. There may be more than one interim payment and there will always be a final payment. Calls to lawyers may be appropriate at this stage, but remember that the final payment from an estate can take a long time. Someone simply needs to have a look at all non-contingent open estates every quarter if possible (*see page 99*). The final resolution is not in your hands and there is little you can do except keep asking for action. Remember, the squeaky wheel gets the grease!

The departed *can* speak

Nonetheless, there is a lot you can do when these estates are completely closed. The valuable information you can get is the last gift these marvelous people give you, and here is what you need to know about the departed. In a report called *The Dead Speak*, they can help you get more legacies from people like them. There are three ways you can make that happen.

1. Analyze Wills

- date of first Will
- date of updates
- date of final Will
- charitable bedfellows (if there are any), as many of your departed will remember more than one charity in their Will
- payment schedule from first notification to closed estate

2. Analyze the departed

On the database

- age at death
- province
- did they tell us (were they a pledger)?
- were they a prospect or suspect?
- how were they recruited?
- what kind of donor were they?
  - monthly active
  - monthly lapsed
  - OTG active
  - OTG lapsed
  - major donor active
  - major donor lapsed
- how much did they leave to charity?
- how much did they leave to bedfellows if any

Not on the database

- age at death
- province
- how much did they leave to charity?
- how much did they leave to bedfellows, if any

False bequesters (those marked as expectancies but who passed on without leaving a gift in their Will)

- how were they recruited?
- what kind of donor were they?
- monthly active
- monthly lapsed
- OTG active
- OTG lapsed
- major donor active
- major donor lapsed

3. Analyze the database

How many people on the database died in the last 5 years?

- how many were pledgers?
- what kind of donors were they?
- how were they recruited?

How many pledgers do you have?

- how were they recruited?
- do you ask pledgers to send back a commitment form?
- how many do you get back?

Have some pledgers sent you a copy of their Will?

How many prospects do you have?

- how were they recruited?

How many suspects do you have?

- how were they recruited

Your departed can give you valuable information about your program, including numbers you can use to project future income growth. When we created *The Dead Speak* report at WWF, here's what we found out about our 380 closed estates:

- 380 people gave us $30,000,000 for a legacy average of $79,000.
- 83% gave less than $5,000 in their lifetime.
- 48% gave less than $1,000 in their lifetime.
- 66% (249) were donors and 32% (131) were non-donors.

Of the 249 donors:

- 32% were monthly donors and 68% were single gift donors.
- Only 20% of these donors told us we were in their Will.

From this tracking information, you can draw conclusions and apply the learning to the real world of today. Most crucially, you can use it to inform your approach to your Pledgers, Prospects and Suspects — your legacy lifeline.

Your *pledgers (or intenders or expectancies)*

These are the kind folks who have told you that they have put your charity in their Will or estate plan. They remain pledgers until they join the departed and that may take a long time. In fact, they're going to do everything in their power to postpone that ultimate gift! This means that you will need to provide them with regular communications that make them feel special — because they are! We will look at this communication when we talk about your *Legacy Love Story (see page 125, Appendix Four)*.

Your *prospects*

The third group you need to track are your prospects. These people have told you in one way or another that they are thinking about or will think about putting your charity in their Will or estate plan. They too will have their own legacy story which you will create in order to turn them into pledgers. Among your prospects are your current and past board, your current and past volunteers and your current and past staff. In legacy giving, the old adage stands, "Family First!"

Your *suspects*

Brainstorm:
Search out and care for your most likely suspects

These are people in your donor file—potentially not even current donors—whom you *think* would consider putting your charity in their Will or estate plan. Monthly donors, loyal one-time donors, recently-lapsed long-time monthly or one-time donors. People like your *departed*. And people who strongly support your charitable bedfellows—the other organizations to which your *departed* left a charitable gift. You just need to be creative and think about who might leave a gift in their Will to your charity. This is another brainstorm opportunity. And of course, these folks will also receive their own Love Story to turn them into prospects or potentially right into pledgers.

While you're tracking your *departed* and caring for your *pledgers*, *prospects* and *suspects*, you can sprinkle your legacy dust everywhere. Recently, the Agents of Good replaced the word "dust" with "glitter". We think the word better captures the creative energy needed to create a legacy communication program to die for! Pun intended! Ask yourself, "How can my organization show *all* our donors that we would welcome them leaving a legacy to our good work?"

Certainly, your newsletter will offer many opportunities for legacy glitter. Get a commitment from the newsletter editors to give legacies one page in every issue. Then work some *Donor Love* magic for legacy pledgers and prospects. A book of remembrance at your office? Some photos of the departed? A catchy tagline for your legacy program? A special welcoming *Legacy Circle* with appropriate benefits? There is much you can do here and, like your Love Story, this is an area where you can clearly distinguish yourselves from the competition.

Brainstorm:
Create an atmosphere of Yes

To do this you need to identify and eliminate the reasons your donors might say "no" to a legacy gift. This is yet another opportunity for a creative brainstorm. Among the excuses for a "no" that you'll find will be "I'm not rich," "My kids wouldn't like it," "I'm not sure I have enough money," and "I don't have a Will." You'll find many more and for each, you can develop a response. (See Holy Sh*t Moment 17 for some very recent Canadian research on barriers.)

Love them to death

Stephen Pidgeon, a respected fundraiser from the UK wrote a book called *How to Love Your Donors to Death*. It's a great read with a simple message — no twaddle. This means that every communication your donors receive should be inspiring, passionate, relevant and personal. Thank you letters that make you smile. Appeals that ignite your passion. Newsletters that talk about what donors make possible. In short, a great legacy program comes out of a great annual program.

It's so easy to say but not easy to do. It needs constant vigilance and blunt conversations to ensure that your standards remain high so that you never find yourself "making do" with approaches and materials that are just not good enough. As the last *Donor Love* principle reminds us (*see page 19*), you need to do the small things right — all the time.

Why love them to death? Simply because at the end of the day your success will depend largely on how well they identify with your mission and its programs. And that in turn will flow from how well you really know and understand them. Here are six important lessons about them that can inform that process and move your legacy program toward success.

1. A legacy gift is about values

Your donors will consider a legacy gift if your mission supports their fundamental values. The decision to make a legacy is not about taxes or financial planning, although those considerations may come later. Another look at our partial list of values at the core of protecting nature (*see page 36*) will show that some of your donors share these values, and their legacy gift to your cause will perpetuate them.

Talking to folks about a legacy gift is not about death. It's not about the end. It is about life. It's about living after you're gone. Research shows that your donors with grandchildren are far less likely to leave a legacy gift. That's because they can pass their core values on to their grandkids. In a way, through them, they live forever.

2. Legacy gifts come from your donor's autobiography

In his wonderful eBook, *Inside the Mind of a Planned Giving Donor*, Dr. Russell James reports on research he did into donor motivation using MRI technology. He learned that when donors are asked about making a bequest (a gift in their Will) two parts of the brain are activated. The first is the *lingual gyrus* which is part of the visual system also activated when dreaming. The second is the *precuneus,* which is where we look at ourselves and create our own autobiography. It is where you are constantly storing your story of you.

This finding has led to the success of online or paper surveys to get donors to consider a legacy gift. In these surveys, donors get a chance to think and talk about themselves, about what is important to them, and about their strong personal connections to a charity's mission. A good survey activates the *precuneus*!

3. Words are important

The diligent Dr. James has also published a couple of short eBooks called *Words that Work* and *Words That Work II*. They report on research that shows that you can increase the success of your legacy program by using some words and avoiding others. For instance, he points out, you should stay away from the phrase "leave a bequest" and instead use the phrase "leave a gift in your Will." These indispensable eBooks are available free from MarketSmart. (www.agentsofgood.org/greengreen).

4. Legacy gifts are about loyalty

Loyalty, not wealth, drives legacy gifts. Of course, donors need to have the capacity to make a legacy gift. With the significant growth in many donor's fixed assets — such as their home — more donors are capable of making this gift. The question of who are your most loyal donors is yet another opportunity for a staff and board brainstorm.

Brainstorm:
Target your most loyal donors

These are the people to whom you are going to want to target your legacy marketing. Here's a short list:

- Long-time one-time donors
- Long-time monthly donors
- All monthly donors
- Long-time volunteers
- All volunteers
- Long-time lapsed one-time donors
- Long-time lapsed monthly donors
- People who return *Change of Address* cards
- People who complain
- Current and past staff
- People who RSVP to events but say "no"

Your completed list will confirm that your major donors are not necessarily your best legacy prospects. Going back to our *fish in the pond* analogy, your best legacy prospects aren't fish that get bigger: those are major gift prospects. Your legacy prospects are the fish that eat all the time!

5. Legacy gifts are about commitment

Your donors likely support many charities. Even your monthly donors will be making monthly gifts to other charities. But as they get older, and especially as they begin to consider making a legacy gift, their charity list gets smaller. The ones at the top are those to which the donor is most committed. To find out how committed your donors are, you need to ask them! Since these donors know you well and hopefully have been treated properly, they will tell you. Go back to Roger Craver's *Retention Fundraising* (*see Appendix Three on page 124*) for more guidance on commitment. It is a significant factor in making a legacy gift.

6. Face-to-face is always best

This is true of all fundraising and especially true of legacy work. The challenge is to have the legacy prospect ask for a meeting. You simply need to find creative ways to make it clear that you would be delighted at any time to talk with a donor about their legacy gift to your charity. Some of the most inspiring conversations I've had over 50 years of talking with donors happened when I had a personal talk about their legacy gift. This is truly a triple win — a win for the donor, a win for the organization, and a win for the fundraiser — YOU!

A LEGACY GIFT PLANNER'S MANTRA

You *never* close the gift
This makes legacy fundraising unique. Earlier we said that *Always Be Closing* is the major gift mantra. This, however, is not the case with a legacy gift. That gift closes when your donor joins the *departed*. So your role with legacy pledgers and prospects is entirely as a support—inspiring, knowledgeable, caring support. It speaks to the need for a compelling Legacy Love Story and a generous sprinkling of legacy glitter…everywhere. As my colleague Richard Radcliffe says: "In legacy fundraising, the only ask you are making is a question."

Get in touch with your core values
You don't want to be speechless if a legacy prospect asks you what *your* core values are. In their search for their own values, they may want to hear yours. Revisit the list of core values on page 36. And for a real challenge, narrow it down to two. At this point, you're ready to talk to a legacy donor or prospect about her or his values.

It is a privilege to do this work
I used to revel in the thought that I could get paid for getting people to support what was most important to me—the protection of nature. I had a job helping people make our shared dream for a green world come true. In legacy giving, you spend time talking with people about making a lasting gift to nature by inviting them to, in a very real way, live forever through their last gift for a healthy planet. Still gives me goosebumps!

CHAPTER ELEVEN

The Four Pillars of a Legacy Program

Now that we have looked at the lessons I have learned about legacy fundraising, let's look at what a comprehensive, strategic legacy program looks like. There are four pillars: measurement, money, people and finding them. But I'm going to start with measurement, which cuts across all four concepts.

PILLAR 1: MEASUREMENT

We talked about the importance of measurement earlier, but because so many organizations won't make the investment a legacy program needs, I'm going to outline how you measure your program. Your results will show that your organization would be crazy to stop investing in legacies. I suggest you update this measurement every month for your team and send it to the big bosses every quarter.

The overall measurement report lives in a detailed Excel spreadsheet (*see figures 21-24*). I have created one for the charity I invented earlier, Climate Action Before It's Too Late (CABITL). You may remember from Chapter 5 on page 32 that the legacy revenue budget was $2 million, and the expense was \$100,000. You can download — and steal! — the spreadsheet at www.agentsofgood.org/greengreen.

Part One: Recording past activity

The first part reports on *past activity*. In our example, I include two years, but if you can, go back four. This report provides overall results from two standpoints: people and money. And of course, we put people first! (*See figure 21*).

Part Two: Reporting current results

The second part tracks the *current year's results*, and once again, we look at people first. We budget how many pledgers, prospects, and suspects we will get in one year, and then express that on a monthly basis. In our example, CANBITL hopes to find 36 pledgers, 60 prospects, and 48 suspects in a year, which translates to 3, 5 and 4 respectively every month.

Then we look at money in exactly the same way. CANBITL hopes to raise \$2 million in a year, which is about \$167,000 per month. I know that legacy revenue does not really come in like this, but it remains the best way to budget and track it.

This section also includes your expense budget annually (\$100,000) and monthly (\$8,333). Finally, this part includes a calculation of cost per dollar raised and return on investment (*see tables 1 and 2, Chapter 5, pages 32 and 33*). Legacy work excels in both these categories so it is wise to show these numbers to the powers that be whenever you can. (*See figure 22*).

OVERALL LEGACY PROGRAM BUDGET REPORT

PART ONE: RECORDING PAST ACTIVITY

2018

DONORS	Target	Actual	Variance
Pledgers	10	9	-1
Prospects	20	21	1
DOLLARS	$1,250,000	$1,500,000	$250,000
EXPENSE		$50,000	
ROI		2900%	
Cost/$		$0.03	

2019

DONORS	Target	Actual	Variance
Pledgers	15	16	1
Prospects	30	28	-2
Suspects	20	21	1
DOLLARS	$1,750,000	$1,800,000	$50,000
EXPENSE		$75,000	
ROI		2300%	
Cost/$		$0.04	

Figure 21: Legacy History Budget

PART TWO: REPORTING CURRENT RESULTS
End of June (6 months into fiscal)

2020

DONORS	Month			Year to date			Year		
	Target for month	Actual for Month	Variance	Target for YTD	Actual for YTD	Variance	Target for year	Actual for year	Variance
Pledgers	3	4	-1	18	15	-3	36	15	-21
Prospects	5	6	-1	30	12	-18	60	12	-48
Suspects	4	3	1	24	26	2	48	26	-22

	Dec 31, 2018	Dec 31, 2019	June 30, 2020
Pledgers	9	25	40
Prospects	21	49	61
Suspects	N/A	21	47

DOLLARS	Month			Year to date			Year		
	Target for month	Actual for Month	Variance	Target for YTD	Actual for YTD	Variance	Target for year	Actual for year	Variance
REVENUE	$166,667	$150,000	$(16,667)	$1,000,000	$800,000	$(200,000)	$2,000,000	$800,000	$(1,200,000)
EXPENSE	$8,333	$7,000	$(1,333)	$50,000	$47,000	$(3,000)	$100,000	$47,000	
ROI		2043%			1602%			1602%	
Cost/$		$0.05			$0.06			$0.06	

Figure 22: Legacy revenue and expense budget

Part Three: Projecting future revenue

The third part is a unique aspect of legacy work and provides impressive information, although its crucial to be clear about the assumptions you make. For instance, as the example does, if you assume you will convince 10% of your prospects to become pledgers, you will need a solid plan for doing that.

This future report will gain strength and relevance when you take a close look at your departeds. Then you can be accurate about how many people didn't tell you that you're in their Will (the factor I use in the example is one in four) and the value of your average legacy gift. (We have assumed the Canadian average in 2019 of $35,000). (*See figure 23*).

Part Four: Tracking Estates

The fourth part monitors and reports on estates. This puts you in a stronger position to take any action you should to get estates closed — to put to work all the money your donor kindly left you. (*See figure 24*).

PART THREE: PROJECTING FUTURE REVENUE

	Dec. 31, 2018	Dec. 31, 2019	June 30, 2020
Pledgers	9	25	40
Prospects	21	50	61
Suspects	N/A	21	47

*** **Future Dollar Assumptions:**

Pledgers x .75 (because 75% of them will do it) x 4 (because for every one we know about, there are 4 more) x $35,000 (average legacy gift)

Prospects/10 (one out of 10 will become a donor) x 4 (see above) x $35,000 (see above)

Suspects/20 (one in 20 will become a donor) x 4 (see above) x $35,000 (see above)

FUTURE DOLLARS *

Pledgers	$4,200,000
Prospects	$854,000
Suspects	$329,000
	$5,383,000

As you will see in Holy Sh*t Moment 18 on page 135, new research in Australia suggests that 65% of pledgers will fulfill their pledge. You could adjust for that here. But I'm optimistic that if treated properly, 75% will do it.

Figure 23: Future legacy revenue budget

PART FOUR: TRACKING ESTATES

Open Estates:	
- Notified of Bequest	15
- Partially Realized	12
	27
Contingent Estates:	2
Total Open Estates:	**29**
New estates in FY 19	5
Closed estates in FY 19	4
New estates in FY 20	3
Closed estates in FY 20	1
New estates in June	1

Figure 24: Estate tracking sheet

PILLAR 2: PEOPLE

Investing in people for growth

The first pillar is your people. Good people are at the heart of your program. I can only hope that with the legacy tsunami approaching, you can convince your bosses to invest in people to support you in the major tasks that need to be done. If you're a small shop, you may have to do them all yourself until you start receiving legacy gifts (As I did in 1982!). Then, once you have proven your case, you can take some of the money raised to invest in getting more gifts by hiring more talented people to perform the four key roles a mature program needs.

Keeping track of estates

First, you'll need someone who knows about your closed and open estates to keep track of the money. For charities with a large program, this is a full-time job. It can be a complicated function, but there are resources out there to help make sure you are doing the right things on the administrative side. The person also keeps the legacy tracking sheets (*see figures 21 - 24*) up-to-date. One excellent source of helpful information is *Planned Giving for Canadians,* available from CAGP on its website and available free of charge with CAGP membership.

The *voice* of your legacy program

Someone else needs to be your legacy champion — whether on your board or your staff — who asks people to leave a legacy. They sign letters and emails, write articles, visit donors whenever possible and provide the consistent voice for your program. In WWF's legacy program this person still is former President Monte Hummel, who has been with WWF-Canada for over 40 years. Donors know and respect Monte. He is an eloquent legacy voice, and of course, he has also left a gift in his Will to WWF.

The *face* of your legacy program

To avoid unexpected bumps in the road, someone experienced and knowledgeable needs to be the *face* of the program. Someone to go to for help, who also visits donors and either knows the answers to virtually any question or who knows how and where to get the answers. Warm, friendly, welcoming and knowledgeable, at WWF, this is Maya Ahmad. You can see both Monte and Maya in their roles by visiting WWF Canada's website. The link is at www.agentsofgood.org/greengreen.

Recruiting new pledgers, prospects and suspects

Finally, you'll want an expert communicator to take charge of marketing and communications — the crucial task of bringing in new legacy pledgers, prospects and suspects (if you don't ask, you don't get!) and then looking after these precious people.

PILLAR 3: MONEY

Celebrate your wins

If people are first, then money must be second. We spoke first about the importance of measuring all aspects of your legacy program. That's because the money won't come until later, and in the meantime your bosses will need to be convinced it's worth the wait! Of course, as our example shows, and as your own legacy projections will show, it is.

So be both dogged and creative about measuring the money. Make sure the whole organization knows when you receive a new notification, and certainly whenever you actually *receive* some money. This is your chance to celebrate these fabulous donors, many of whom you will have looked after for a long time. Above all, remember that the money you bring in today will ensure the long-term investment this program needs for tomorrow.

PILLAR 4: FINDING THEM

Finding Them — Where to look

The third pillar in your program is *finding* them. The first step in finding legacy prospects is knowing where to look! You begin with your most loyal donors, however you choose to define them. At the end of that early research, you'll have identified a group of donors who are ready — whether or not they know it! — to be asked properly to make a legacy gift. The great news is that there is no real magic here. Depending on how these donors have been communicating with you in the past, you will either write, email or phone them with an invitation.

Writing works well

Donors who prefer the mail will get a letter, and there are at least three possibilities here. In all cases, these letters are as personal as possible. These are your best donors so you'll be personal with them. The three possible letters are: an invitation to complete a survey, an opportunity to think more carefully about a legacy gift, and an invitation to receive a phone call about a legacy gift.

Start with a letter and a survey

An ideal way to move the connection forward is to introduce a short survey with a letter. I provide an example of the mailed survey in *figure 25*. You can see the whole package at www. agentsofgood.org/greengreen.

The letter should be warm and friendly, and the survey should open with a few questions that encourage donors to think about their relationship with your mission and your charity. Of course, near the end of the survey, you will ask the magic question. Here's an example.

Figure 25: Mailed legacy survey
Credit: WWF-Canada

8. To ensure a vibrant future for wildlife, we will be asking donors to consider creating a charitable gift for the conservation of wildlife and wild places through WWF-Canada in their Will. After you have provided for your loved ones, would you consider leaving a gift in your Will to WWF-Canada?

> *1 [ ] Yes, I would consider making such a legacy gift*
>
> *2 [ ] I have already made provision for a gift in my Will to WWF-Canada*
>
> *3 [ ] I have already made WWF-Canada a beneficiary of another type of legacy gift*
>
> *4 [ ] I am unsure at this time*
>
> *5 [ ] No*

The responses to this survey will begin to build your legacy lifeline. Those whose say "yes" to option one are *prospects*. Those who say "yes" to option two or three are *pledgers*. And those who say "yes" to option four or five are your legacy *suspects*.

A long letter with a shorter survey

This can be a long, personal, passionate, reflective, mission-filled letter. I provide an example in *figure 26*. The short survey is enclosed with this letter. You can see the whole package at www.agentsofgood.org/greengreen:

> *I want to share my passion for nature with the next generation by leaving a gift for the future.*
>
> *1 [ ] I have already included WWF-Canada in my Will.*
>
> *2 [ ] I'm thinking about making a gift in my Will.*
>
> *3 [ ] I would welcome the opportunity to talk with you further about this type of gift. Please contact me at [_____].*

4 [ ] *I don't think that a gift in my Will is the right choice for me at this time.*

All information received will be confidential and without obligation.

Thank You!

Once again, the responses to this survey will help you build your legacy lifeline of pledgers, prospects, and suspects.

A warm, attractive package with the maple key emblem, symbol of Canada's national tree, acting as an intriguing involvement device.

Figure 26: Legacy long letter
Credit: The Nature Conservancy of Canada

Some charities use mail-phone programs

An approach that combines powerful direct mail with expert follow-up phone calls can be effective and has been widely used by used by many charities. Inspired by the work of Ken Ramsay, two Canadian consulting firms, including Legacy Leaders and PG*growth*, have developed this combination to the point that it can generate impressive results. In fact, if the phone is a major part of your annual program and your database is in the tens of thousands, then indeed, this is how your donors might prefer to be contacted. There are also agencies that specialize in talking to older donors about a legacy gift. One is Ottawa-based Keys 360 Marketing, which has had great success.

In my experience, for donors who are used to direct mail, the long letter (*see figure 26*) is the best first option. If you have never asked your donors before to consider a legacy gift, you will get great results with a long letter. The response will launch you on the road of looking after them and will trigger the creation of two important documents, the *why* brochure and the *how* letter. After you use the long letter a few times, about 18 months apart, then you can send the shorter survey. Or solicit these folks with your online survey.

Finding them online with a survey

Did you know that your top legacy prospects are online? Online is a great way to engage these folks in their own way and at their own time, and the most effective online method is sending an email that invites them to take an online survey. I have provided an example of this approach in *figure 27*, and the result will be the continued building of your legacy lifeline.

Figure 27: Invitation to take an online legacy survey
Credit: WWF-Canada

Here is the key survey question which, in one shot gives you pledgers, prospects, and suspects. Significantly, this is question six, not question one, because you need to warm your donors up a bit before asking this important question. Let them first get in touch with their story of themselves. You can see the whole package at www.agentsofgood.org/greengreen.

1 *[ ] Many people like to leave a gift to charity in their Will or estate plan. Have you considered making such a gift to WWF-Canada to benefit Canada's wildlife?*

2 *[ ] I have already left a gift for WWF-Canada in my will or estate plan.*

3 [ ] *I am interested in making this type of gift to WWF-Canada.*

4 [ ] *Not now, but in the future I would definitely be interested in making this type of gift to WWF-Canada.*

5 [ ] *Not now, but in the future, I might possibly be interested in making this type of gift to WWF-Canada.*

6 [ ] *I am not interested in this type of gift.*

The breakdown here is slightly different. Those who choose number 2 are *pledgers*. Those who choose number 1 or 3 are *prospects*. Those who choose number 4, 5, or 6 are *suspects*.

Finding them on social media

As so many of your legacy prospects are online, social media programs such as Facebook, Twitter and Instagram can help you build your legacy lifeline, and I have included a couple of examples (*see figures 28 and 29*).

Figure 28: Facebook legacy ad
Credit: Peterborough Humane Society

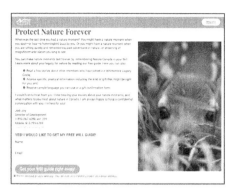

Figure 29: Facebook legacy ad
Credit: Nature Canada

Of course, social media is also where people who are not your donors can hear about leaving a legacy for your good work. Remember, *WWF had no record of one-third of the people who remembered wildlife in their Will.*

In summary, depending on how much of a budget you have, with even a small audience to talk to and an idea of their communication preferences, you can use these techniques to build a robust legacy lifeline quickly. The only question will be how much front-end money your organization is willing to invest to find these donors, recognizing that although this activity offers a truly outstanding medium- and long-term investment opportunity, it will likely lose money in the short term.

Converting prospects and suspects

A unique aspect of legacy marketing is that you are constantly working to convert your prospects and suspects into pledgers. And even once they are pledgers, your job is still not over. In fact in many ways it has only just begun. While some of your pledgers — bless them — will tell you they intend to put you in their Will, this is still only their *intention*. Some research suggests that donors won't actually put your charity in their

Will until after they turn 80. At about that time, they begin to feel the cold wind of mortality. They find themselves going to more funerals, and their doctor may even suggest they get their affairs in order.

To cope with this uncertainty, some charities ask those who pledge that they'll make a gift in their Will or estate plan to send back a form filled out with the specifics of their legacy gift. I find this non donor-centred and even intrusive. And don't forget, in any case, most of the people who will leave a gift in their Will never tell you. At WWF, only 1 in 5 people told us. Nothing speaks more strongly to the importance of an ongoing legacy glitter program than this single fact.

This means that the real challenge in your legacy program is not getting pledgers. You have to do all you can to *confirm* the pledge. Your pledgers need a passionate, thoughtful, personal, and inspiring stream of communications from the voice and the face of your program. As we did with the communication stream in your annual program, we call this their Love Story only this time, it's a *Legacy Love Story*. (*See Appendix Four on page 125*).

If you want to be thorough, you will need three legacy love stories. They can have many things in common, but there will be subtle differences between your pledger love story, your prospect love story, and your suspect love story. Why? Simply because the objective is different for each of the three groups. You want your pledgers to go to their lawyer and write your charity into their Will. You want your prospects to become pledgers; and you want your suspects to become pledgers or prospects. Moving them to action involves a different strategy in each case.

Getting your pledgers to the lawyer

This is the single most challenging part of a strategic legacy program, to which there are no simple solutions. One exciting new initiative being launched nationally in Canada in 2021, called *Willpower,* is modelled on successful programs in the UK and Australia. The goal: to increase the number of Canadians who put a charity in their Will from the current 5% to 8.5% in ten years. That sounds modest, but would be in fact a 60% increase over the current level, and would raise an additional $40 billion for Canadian charitable efforts. For more information about this campaign from the Canadian Association of Gift Planners, follow link at www.agentsofgood.org/greengreen.

A great start for your own pledger stewardship program (aka. legacy glitter!) is to develop your own powerful, well-planned *Legacy Pledgers Love Story* for a calendar year, and one possible approach is shown in Appendix Four. (In all cases when they receive the regular mailings, they will be recognized as a legacy pledger.) You will notice a similarity between this and the annual *Donor Love* story… and why not? Your legacy pledgers that you know about are active donors. Indeed, research shows that once annual donors become legacy pledgers, their annual donation increases by as much as 30%! Of course, you will invite these donors to opt out of these communications. But you will find, as long as they are written with *Donor Love,* few will exercise this option. In fact, if many do, it's time to check the quality of what you are sending them!

This is a good time to consider whether your legacy program needs a name. People don't make legacy gifts to be part of a group, but anyone considering making a gift likes to know that they are not alone…that other people, just like them, have taken the same step. So a catchy name and attractive simple logo is a good idea. For WWF in the US and Canada, folks join the *Legacy Circle.* Here is the simple logo incorporating of course the world-famous panda logo (*see figure 30*).

Figure 30: WWF uses this logo in the US and Canada
for its legacy donors
Credit: WWF-Canada

Getting prospects to become pledgers

Donors who have shown an interest need to be moved to make the commitment. And we know now they will not be moved by talking about tax advantages and financial planning. They will be moved by their emotions, and to do this, you need to create a *Why* brochure, the package you send to prospects to turn them into pledgers, along with a friendly, welcoming letter from the face of the program (*see figure 31*).

This short, snappy letter makes three points: first, thanks for considering this special gift; second, I'm here to help; and third, what you tell us will be held in strict confidence. Here's what a *Why* brochure looks like (*see figure 32*).

legacy
circle

Monday, May 28, 2018

Mr. David Love

Dear Mr. Love,

♫ "Summertime and the livin' is easy

Fish are jumpin' and the cotton is high" ♫

This is one of my favourite songs from George Gershwin's opera, Porgy and Bess, written in 1935.

Fishing has been a big part of my life. As a boy growing up in northern Ontario, I used to show people where to catch pike and walleye on the English River, and for 10 cents a fish, I'd filet them for them.

Later, I served as canoe and fishing guide on most of the big rivers tumbling down off the Shield into James and Hudson Bay. Feeling the throb of the current against your waders is still a pretty good way to experience Canada.

Even if you're not into fishing, I do hope you get out this summer to enjoy Canada's waterways, be they oceans, rivers lakes or even a small pond. Often, these bodies of water attract wildlife too!

Once again, I'm delighted to enclose your summer newsletter. In it, you will read about dedicated people from coast to coast to coast helping wildlife thrive. Folks making highways safer for wildlife; folks monitoring caribou populations; folks recording whale sounds; folks looking at polar bear and human conflicts. And this is just a short list. You can read more in your newsletter.

Figure 31: Letter mailed with newsletter to legacy donors
Credit: WWF-Canada

Figure 32: Oak Ridges Moraine Land Trust *Why* brochure
Credit: Agents of Good

You can see the whole brochure at www.agentsofgood.org/greengreen.

Your *why* brochure shares stories of donors who have remembered you in their will, or stories that demonstrate the impact of legacy giving. It resonates with shared values, demonstrates those values in action through the impact of legacy gifts, establishes your effectiveness and efficiency and invites a personal conversation.

Look for three kinds of stories:

1. People who have passed away and you have done something amazing with their gift. This story is most impactful when told by a living relative who can both express their own thoughts and feelings and also relate those of the departed.

2. Donors who have remembered you in their Will and are prepared to talk about why, how it makes them feel and what they hope for the future.

3. Someone close to the organization — a board chair, long-serving volunteer or staff member who has remembered you in their Will. She/he can talk about her/his trust and confidence in the future vision and effectiveness of your organization.

You don't need all three at any one time, but these are the types of stories you will want to continue to gather as your program grows.

The How letter—moving from emotion to action

Along with your *why* brochure, you need a *how* letter. While emotion will spark the commitment, hard-headed reason is crucial to seal the deal. Your *how* letter provides some specific (but donor-friendly) information about the various kinds of legacy gifts that are possible, the pros and cons of different approaches, and sample wording for clauses to be inserted in a Will. In *figure 33*, I provide an example of an excellent *How* letter from the Oak Ridges Moraine Land Trust. You can see the whole letter at www.agentsofgood.org/greengreen.

Thank you for your interest in taking action to protect nature forever with a gift in your Will to the Oak Ridges Moraine Land Trust. This document is meant to support you and the professionals helping you through this process. We hope it also helps guide conversations with your loved ones.

Creating or updating your Will takes time and effort, but it is important and fulfilling. As a key part of your estate plan, your Will lets you decide with whom you want to share your assets. Your Will is the ultimate expression of the values and beliefs you hold in life. It is about your interests and passions, not merely your assets.

Your Will is an opportunity to reflect on what matters most to you. And you can support the work of a charity—like our Land Trust—*and* your loved ones. In fact, a gift in your Will can provide tax benefits that are passed on to your heirs. Your charitable designation can be claimed against 100% of net income on the final two lifetime tax returns. In short, a gift to our Land Trust could increase your gift left for loved ones. Your professional advisor can provide you with more guidance.

What we provide for you here is not intended to replace legal advice and none of these forms are legally binding. But they can help you—and us—plan for the future.

You are welcome to contact me for more information about legacy giving, to submit completed forms, or for a confidential conversation about including our Land Trust in your legacy plans. It's always wonderful to hear stories about what nature has meant to our most loyal and cherished donors so please don't hesitate to connect with me at any time.

Thank you for your ongoing and vital support of our Land Trust.

Yours, for nature, forever

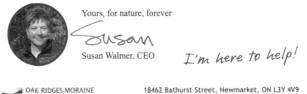

Susan Walmer, CEO   *I'm here to help!*

OAK RIDGES MORAINE LAND TRUST

18462 Bathurst Street, Newmarket, ON L3Y 4V9
905-853-3171 | **oakridgesmoraine.org**
Charitable Registration #87320 8920

Figure 33: Oak Ridges Moraine Land Trust How letter
Credit: Agents of Good

Of course, your prospects are offered the *why* brochure and the *how* letter as needed. I often use a special mailing or email offering them in November. This leads us to your *Legacy Prospects Love Story*, which looks the same as the *Pledgers Love Story*, but adds special elements for prospects. The most important — I suggest in May — is an invitation, in the mail or online, to move from prospect to pledger.

Getting suspects to become prospects or pledgers

If you recruit and keep track of suspects, you need to do something with them! The best idea is simply to create your *Legacy Suspects Love Story,* which looks like your other Love Stories, but with special additions to turn suspects into pledgers or prospects. This could simply be the May invitation you create for prospects.

The power of your website

The fact that most of your legacy pledgers, prospects and suspects are online means that a great legacy website can work wonders. It can get your pledgers to the lawyer (**job one**!); and it can move your prospects and suspects into pledgers. At WWF, we took a two-pronged approach. First, from the WWF homepage under the DONATE heading, we have a legacy section called *A Gift in Your Will* (http://www.wwf.ca/donate/legacy/). But in recognition of the importance of the role of the website in WWF's legacy marketing program, and because we contact so many legacy pledgers, prospects and suspects electronically, we developed a special website dedicated solely to legacies (https://mylegacyforwildlife.org).

This concludes our look at legacy fundraising. Even as I write this, new research is available to help you do it better. Take the time to learn and apply this research. Your best donors, and many others you don't know about, are looking to make the most significant gift they will make in their lifetime.

Legacy fundraising will dominate the fundraising world for the next thirty years for all the reasons I mentioned earlier (*see page 71*). And I suspect that most of the talk will be about the money. How much there is. How many people have it? Who has it?

But legacy work is the pinnacle of donor-centered fund-raising—the core of *Donor Love*. That's because while money is obviously a crucial ingredient, this is really all about your precious supporters who have travelled to the end of their journey with you. Now they want to make a final gift. A gift which perpetuates their fundamental values. A gift that lets them live on. How much money they have and how much they might leave you is not only irrelevant, it's none of your business.

Your business is to hold their hand as they take those last steps.

Legacies are about life. Live well. Love well. Leave well.

Go forth and do likewise.

A Final Word

When I began my career in 1969, many fundraisers like me really didn't know what we were doing. We didn't know what worked and what didn't. That, happily, is no longer true. Fund-raising giants along the way have shown us how to do our life-saving work. And they have shared their secrets, some of which are in this book.

You have read about the importance of "Asking Properly." There is no excuse anymore to ask *improperly*. No excuse to create appeals that are organization-centered, predictable, staid, and boring. No more appeals that treat our donors like ATM machines. Now we know how to create appeals that are donor-centered, innovative, passionate, and exciting, and that treat our donors as heroes with love.

Women and men who are raising money to restore nature have the most important and most satisfying job in the world. If you are one of these lucky people, I hope the information in this book helps you do your life-saving job better.

Appendix One:
List of Brainstorms

Throughout this book, you will see this graphic ☀. It indicates an opportunity for you to brainstorm with your colleagues. These are the eight opportunities to brainstorm. You can do this with whomever you think will help you finalize the product. My experience is that often those not directly connected to the topic have valuable things to say. Everyone in your organization is committed to achieving your mission.

Your Charity's Values (page 36)
Greatest Hits   (page 81)
Fondest Dreams   (page 81)
Future Vision   (page 81)
Possible Suspects   (page 86)
Atmosphere of "Yes"   (page 87)
Most Loyal Donors   (page 90)

Appendix Two: What Makes a Great Boss

As it turned out, I found out along the way that raising money for nature is really hard work, even when you have mastered the systems, procedures, approaches and techniques that you'll find in this book. In fact, none of that technical learning will be of any use unless you are part of a team seized by the mission and directed by *inspired leadership*.

Usually, fundraisers report to a boss who either makes our job easier or harder. I was blessed to work with great bosses throughout my fundraising career, and over the years have noticed the things your boss needs to do to support you — the elements that define that inspired leadership — so before we move on to the details, I'll share a few tips on what I've come to look for in a team that can truly soar. (I'm going to assume your boss is a woman, and I'm assuming a small shop, so your boss is the president or executive director.)

1. **First, and most important, she needs a searing conservation vision.** Whether it is a small idea or a big one, your boss has to give you something *brilliant* to sell.

2. **Your boss needs to be ahead of the curve.** She needs to see what's coming in the fundraising world and how to prepare for it. Today, this means your boss needs to be a champion of donor-centred fundraising. She has to put donors first.

3. **She needs to take risks.** Your boss should demand that you prepare a solid case for investment, and then she should be ready to act.

4. **She should be fearless.**

5. **She needs great fundraising instincts.**

6. **She needs to be a delightful, if sometimes challenging collaborator.** You will raise millions of dollars for *Nature* by communicating with your donors. Your boss needs to make your appeals better. More honest. More direct. More conservation-focussed.

7. **Finally, she needs to be a huge ally for fundraising.** She needs to know that if you're going to have the best conservation program in the country, you'll need the best fundraising campaigns and the best fundraising people in the country. She will need to champion the work fundraisers do...from the major gift person asking for $1 million to the donor care person on the phone changing a mailing address.

So whether you're the leader yourself, scrambling at the entry level, head-down in the largest, most demanding campaign of your career, or looking for your next challenge, keep this short list in mind as you follow your own path for *Nature*.

Appendix Three: Standing on the Shoulders of Giants

Here are ten fundraising books which have helped me raise more money for nature.

Asking Properly, George Smith, White Lion Press Ltd, 1996

Thank You, Penelope Burk, Burk and Associates Ltd, 2000

Relationship Fundraising, Ken Burnett, Jossey-Bass, 2002

Hidden Gold, Harvey McKinnon, Taylor Trade Publishing, 2003

30 Letters that Changed the World, Steve Thomas, McThat Press, 2012

Retention Fundraising: The New Arts and Science of Keeping Your Donors for Life, Roger Craver, Emerson & Church Publishers, 2014

Why Legacies are Brilliant for Charities and How to Get Them, Richard Radcliffe, Smee & Ford, 2017

Engagement Fundraising, Greg Warner, MarketSmart, 2018

If Only You'd Known, Tom Ahern, Emerson Church, 2019

You Can't Take It With You, Fraser Green, Holly Wagg, Charlotte Field, Goodworks Communications Inc, 2019

Appendix Four: Sample Legacy Pledger Love Story

January 21: Renewal mailing one

February 25: Legacy thank you

March 9: Spring newsletter. I assume you can convince your newsletter editors to give your program at least one page per issue. This works to make your current pledgers feel great. I also assume you can either mail or email this so it comes personally from the voice of your program. (See a sample letter from WWF in *figure 31.*)

April 12: Short thank you videos from the field, adapted for legacy pledgers

April 22: Earth Day Voice broadcast thank you adapted for legacy pledgers

May 4: *Leave a Legacy* message — May is "Leave a Legacy Month" Invitation to special events

May 20: Spring special appeal

June 15: Summer event — Events have even more power in

your legacy program than in your other fundraising activities. The WWF pledger and prospect event described earlier on page 53 is always oversubscribed and thoroughly enjoyed by all. We also had great success with financial planning events that were more about life than finances.

Finally, consider inviting your legacy pledgers to wear a coloured ribbon at events to which they're invited, and, at some point during the event, recognize them. This will not only make them feel special but play to the importance of social norming. "Hey, she looks just like me. Maybe I should leave a legacy gift too."

June 24: Summer Newsletter

August 17: Town Hall on an important currant topic

Sept 7: Fall Special Appeal

Sept 21: Fall Newsletter

Oct 12: Fall Event

Nov 1: Preview of *Philanthropy Day* in mid-November

Dec 8: Year-end Thanks

In your legacy donor hierarchy, looking after your pledgers is your first priority, so make their experience with your mission second to none. As a dear colleague once not-to-subtly suggested to me, "David. Why should we spend all this money recruiting folks to be passengers on the Titanic? Surely we should make our donor experience the best in the world before we work to find new donors." Why indeed! Your legacy pledger experience needs to be superlative.

Appendix Five: David Love's Holy Sh*t Moments

The area of legacy fundraising is undergoing dramatic change. As the "legacy tsunami" approaches, new research around the world will help you ask for legacy gifts "properly."

These Holy Sh*t Moments capture research which leads to entirely fresh insights. Of course, **the trick is to do something about them**. The author would be delighted with any examples!

Holy Sh*t Moment 1

One pledger in four increased their intention to leave a charitable bequest when given the option to "honour a friend or family member by making a memorial gift to charity in my last will and testament."

In *Words that Work* by Russell James, Director of Graduate Studies in Charitable Financial Planning at Texas Tech University, learned from his research that bequest donors respond well to socially normative language, testimonials from living people, and rousing memories of loved ones.

James' new research in *Words that Work II* shows us that one in four people increased their intention to leave a gift in their will if they could "honour a friend or family member by making a memorial gift to charity in my last will and testament." This works when they can honour an ascendant (someone older than them) who is female (such as their grandmother). It is helpful to have check boxes, where they have the option to state that they'd like to leave a bequest in tribute or in honour of someone, and several lines to write in that person's name and their relationship.

Holy Sh*t Moment 2

People don't buy what you do. They buy why you do it.

In his TED talk, Simon Sinek identifies a pattern among leaders and companies that achieve greatness. They all communicate the *why* of their work, before they communicate the how and the what. Describing what he calls *The Golden Circle*, Sinek argues that people don't buy what you do, they buy why you do it. What you do simply serves as proof of what you believe. For this reason, it is important to do business with the people who believe what you believe. Like the precious folks in your legacy lifeline.

Holy Sh*t Moment 3

The boomers are coming. They will leave legacy gifts and they are a diverse group.

Recent research by Fraser Green confirms that Baby Boomers are going to be excellent legacy candidates. These 9.1 million Canadians are a very diverse group. In his charming book *Stayin Alive,* Michael Adams breaks boomers down into four different tribes: Disengaged Darwinists (4.4 million – 48%), Connected Enthusiasts (1.9 million – 21%), Autonomous Rebels (1.7 million – 19%) and Anxious Communitarians (1.1

million – 12%). To engage these people in a legacy conversation, we need to recognize their diversity, and speak to them in a way that recognizes their unique cultural perspective.

Holy Sh*t Moment 4

Legacy giving is inspired by the autobiographical part of the brain.

Obsessed by why people make a legacy gift, the tireless Russell James, author of the *Words that Work* eBooks, put donors into MRI machines and asked them questions about giving to charity. He was *not* surprised to see that the part of the brain that lit up when talking about donations was the part about giving back. About feeling an obligation towards others. He *was* surprised, however, to learn that when thinking about a legacy gift, an entirely different region of the brain came alive — the autobiographical section, the part that keeps track of the story of ourselves! (*See pages 127 and 133*).

Holy Sh*t Moment 5

Research by Emily Smith and Jennifer Aaker shows that the happy life and the meaningful life differ.

The surest path to true happiness, they conclude, lies in chasing not just happiness but also a meaningful life. In fact, the pursuit of happiness can negatively affect our well-being. Their research in early 2017 found that meaningful lives share three features:

- *Purpose*, the degree to which you feel directed and motivated by valued life goals;
- *Comprehension*, the ability to understand and make sense of your life experiences and weave them into a coherent whole; and
- *Mattering*, the belief that your existence is significant and valued.

When people say their lives are meaningful, it's because they feel their lives have purpose, coherence and worth. This thought is also profoundly captured in two other must-read books, *Man's Search for Meaning*, and *Yes To Life In Spite of Everything* by Victor Frankl.

Holy Sh*t Moment 6

In Derek Sivers' book, *Anything You Want*, he points out that ideas are just a multiplier of execution.

Awful idea	= -1
Weak idea	= 1
So—so idea	= 5
Good idea	= 10
Great idea	= 15
Brilliant idea	= 20
No execution	= $1
Weak execution	= $1,000
So—so execution	= $10,000
Good execution	= $100,000
Great execution	= $1,000,000
Brilliant execution	= $10,000,000

A brilliant idea with no execution is worth $20. The most brilliant idea with brilliant execution is worth $200 million. A good idea with good execution is worth $1 million. Ideas are worthless unless they are well executed.

Holy Sh*t Moment 7

When lawyers or financial planners prompt their clients to include a charity in their Will, it has a dramatic effect.

Research in the UK in 2013 showed that if lawyers or financial planners do not prompt a gift, 4.9% of people put a charity in their Will. But if they ask, "Would you like to leave any money to charity in your Will?" 10.8% of them take that step. And if they say, "Many of our clients like to leave money to charity in their Will. Are there any causes you're passionate about?" 15.4% of people put a charity in their Will.

Holy Sh*t Moment 8

MarketSmart developed an excellent list of eleven best practices for looking after your pledgers.

1. **Survey them.** There's simply no better way to cost-effectively conduct donor discovery.

2. **Rank them.** You only have so much time, and since 80% of your legacy gift dollars will come from 20% of your legacy society members, you must determine who it most likely to do it.

3. **Be relevant.** Now that you understand them (thanks to the survey), you should use the information they gave you about why they planned their gift, their interests and their passions so you can send them communications that matter to them, not you.

4. **Personalize everything.** Use their names and spell them correctly! It's just plain nice to do so and you owe them that courtesy.

5. **Create an Alumni feeling.** "You are part of a special club and you are special because you're in it."

6. **Include testimonials.** Social proof is powerful. Don't forget that!

7. **Drive them online.** Digital communications are cheap!

8. **Make them feel like a hero.** "You are amazing because you have planned an amazing gift that will help others in the future."

9. **Prove impact.** "Here's where your money goes (and will go)."

10. **Include conversion opportunities.** Make it easy for them to contact you (give them your direct phone number or email, not info@), make it easy for them to sign up for volunteer opportunities, and help them learn about and consider ways they can add to the gift they already planned.

11. **Call and visit them!** Many donors leave several organizations in their wills. If you don't visit them, another almost certainly will. Then the gift for your organization might disappear!

Holy Sh*t Moment 9
The third act
The irrepressible Jane Fonda talks about *The Third Act* in this 11-minute Ted Talk: https://www.ted.com/talks/jane_fonda_life_s_third_act/transcript#t-660839

Holy Sh*t Moment 10
The three deaths
In *Sum,* neuroscientist-by-day and fiction-writer-by-night David Eagleman, says we die three times. We die the first time when our breath leaves our body. We die the second time when our loved ones return our body to the ground. And our third and final death is a moment, sometime in the future, when our name is spoken for the last time. Of course, this means as legacy fundraisers, we help prolong our donors' lives.

Holy Sh*t Moment 11
Donor conversations
Donors are eager to talk about their legacy, and here are some tips to guide these conversations. It is a conversation; not an interview. Personalize where they live, how they give and any other details. And ask them:

- about their first love of your cause;
- about their fondest memories associated with your cause;
- if their interest was sparked by another person — grandma, uncle?
- what your priorities for action *now* should be;
- what your priorities for action *in the future* should be;
- "Are we making progress?"
- "Have you put us in your Will?"
- "Are you thinking about putting us in your Will?"
- "What do your loved ones think?"
- "How would you like to see your gift used?"

Holy Sh*t Moment 12
The importance of stewardship

In a report *Understanding Legacy Stewardship* from Legacy Foresight in the UK, there are ten learnings about stewardship from over twenty charities. The top three are:

1. Stewardship is an area in which you can distinguish yourself from other charities;

2. Think creatively about your assets — what can you provide donors which is unique to you; and

3. The best stewardship conveys magic!

Holy Sh*t Moment 13
Neuroscience

As fundraisers, we justly celebrate when we learn something new that helps us do our job better and create value for our precious donors to accomplish our charity's mission. Led by researchers such as Russell James, whose MRI studies revolutionized the way we market legacies, we continue to learn more about how our brains work.

Recently, new studies are showing us how our brains work when we make donations to charity. These learnings about anchoring, social norming, framing, cognitive dissonance, and more will help us find ways to encourage our donors to give more. We should embrace this new science with enthusiasm, but new knowledge about donor motivation is not a replacement for one-on-one human relationships and no excuse to create boring, organization-centered, confusing appeals. In everything we do, the donor comes first.

Holy Sh*t Moment 14
In Memory Gifts
Recent research in the UK by the folks at Legacy Foresight tells us that people who make a gift in memory of someone are excellent legacy prospects. We know that an in-memory gift can bring great benefits, both to a donor and to the charity, including focus and a therapeutic outlet for grief; a new reason to get in touch; and the inspiration for continued engagement. But there is also now hard evidence to show that an in-memory relationship with a charity may also lay the foundation for a legacy gift.

Holy Sh*t Moment 15
Reactive and reflective Will making
In the midst of the COVID-19 crisis, Goodworks hosted an intriguing webinar on legacy marketing during the pandemic. Among the gems of knowledge shared was the discovery that writing or updating a Will is traditionally a reflective process. People think about it for a while before they do it. But the pandemic found that many people were doing these things quickly, without much forethought.

Holy Sh*t Moment 16
Legacy marketing in times of crisis
What should we do when our world, and more importantly,

our donors' world is turned upside down, as happened when the coronavirus paralyzed all global human activity? My colleague and legacy guru Ligia Pena offers some great advice in a webinar she did in April, 2020. Here's the link to it: https://globetrottingfundraiser.com/resources/.

Holy Sh*t Moment 17
Brand-new Canadian research looks at the barriers to people leaving a gift in their Will
To prepare for the Willpower campaign, CAGP undertook some research into why people don't leave a gift in their Will. They identified three:

1. They want to leave a gift to their loved ones. They don't think they can do this *and* leave a gift to charity in their Will.

2. They can't decide which charity they support they should leave a gift in their Will to.

3. They haven't talked with their loved ones about leaving a gift to charity in their Will.

Organizations need to find ways to strategically address these barriers

Holy Sh*t Moment 18
Brand-new research in Australia suggest that as many as 35% of those who said they left a gift in their Will DON'T!
The biggest take-away from this is that 65% DO IT! So keep marketing those legacies!

He looked at 700 "departed" from 10 charities. He also looked at prospects (only 11% did it) and suspects (5% did it).

He also found that when people receive information from the charity, the number who don't do it significantly decreases. So keep sending great stuff and sprinkling legacy glitter!

Appendix Six: David's Fundraising Alphabet

26 Words from 51 Years in Service of Donors

One word for each letter of the alphabet, taking us right to the core of great fundraising. It inspired by the late Tony Elischer, another giant upon whose shoulders I stood. Tony was brilliant, funny, and above all passionate about great fundraising and about finding and developing young talent around the world. Every time I met him, I left inspired to do my fundraising work better.

On to my alphabet.

A = Authentic
Our fundraising needs to ring true. It needs to be honest, genuine, respectful, and trustworthy.

B = Bold
Our donor heroes want to work with us to make their world a better place. This is no time to be timid. It calls for boldness.

C = Creative
Say something worth saying in a different way. Have a bird write a letter. Have a monthly donor write the thank you letter.

D = Donor
Bless the men and women who give time, talent, and treasure to causes they deeply care about. The blessed unrest.

E = Emotional
"This problem makes me angry and I want to help." Donors' emotions drive their giving. Kindle their emotions so they will continue the journey with you.

F = Future
Our donors yearn for a better future. A world of justice. A world of safety. A world of health. A green world.

G = Gratitude
We can't say thank you too often. Think of different ways to show gratitude. Communicate without asking for money. Make donors feel like insiders.

H = Hero
Our donors are heroes. They make what we do possible. Celebrate them. Invite them to tell their stories. Share their hero stories.

I = Innovation
Find new ways to excite donors about your work. Have different people tell your story. Turn your challenges into opportunities.

J = Journey
Create meaningful, fulfilling, and successful journeys. Provide plenty of options to take more personal paths,

K = Knowledge
Keep current. Learn every day. As David Ogilvy said, "We prefer the discipline of knowledge to the anarchy of ignorance."

L = Love
Love drives the philanthropic spirit. Your donors love what you do. Try to find ways to love them back.

M = Money
In the end, this is what we want. But to get it, we don't talk about money. Because money follows value!

N = Network
You are surrounded by colleagues doing your important work. Reach out to them. Challenge them. Learn from them.

O = Optimism
Our donors are optimists. They believe that with you, they can make a difference. Find shining ways to show them that they are right.

P = Passion
Passion is at the heart of accomplishing our mission. Passion drives your donors. Make passion radiate from your communications.

Q = Question
Our donors deserve lively, personal answers to these questions: What are you going to do? Why now? Why You? Why me? Where will my money go?

R = Risk
Every once in a while, take a risk. Try something new? Say something provocative. Send something completely different.

S = Solution
Our donors don't come to us to hear about problems. They come to us for solutions that sparkle.

T = Trust
We earn our donors' trust by treating them well, by listening to their concerns, by inviting their stories.

U = Urgency
Genuine urgency drives action. Fake urgency (year-end tax-receipt mailings, annual fund drives) create apathy.

V = Vulnerable
There is immense value in vulnerable and emotional conversations now more than ever before.

W = Will
At the end of their journey with us, our donors remember what matters most to them in their Will. A gift that lasts forever.

X = Xerox
Copy everything! You can see examples of great success all around you. Read about fundraising success by checking out www.sofii.org.

Y = You
The most important word in fundraising. Great things happen when we make the subtle shift from "What We Do" to "What You Make Possible."

 Z = Zero tolerance
For incompetent, ignorant, insensitive fundraising

Appendix Seven:
Four Legacy Visions

Oak Ridges Moraine Land Trust

In 2040, the Oak Ridges Moraine Land Trust will treasure two groups of angels. The first are far-sighted landowners on the moraine who are eager to protect it. The second are those generous donors who contribute money so that the land trust can look after these precious gems forever.

Interval House

In 2040, Interval House will continue to be a refuge for woman and children escaping domestic violence. But we hope this is an uncommon occurrence. Interval House will always be there for women who are looking to rebuild their lives.

Nature Canada

Our vision is a future where Canada's magnificent natural heritage is preserved, explored and adored by our children, our grandchildren and for generations to come

Ontario Nature

Our vision is a future where nature in your backyard, our boreal forest and beyond is protected, forever.

A Pandemic Afterword

This book was written, edited, published and marketed during the COVID-19 pandemic. To not talk about it and fundraising for nature seems myopic. There are two things I'd like to say.

The first is that the pandemic confirms the essential thesis of *Green, Green*. We have perhaps two generations to stop the destruction of the natural world before it destroys us. Sorry folks, it's that simple.

We need to raise magnitudes more money to heal and restore nature. And we need an army of great fundraisers to do that.

Second, we now know how to "ask properly." Donors, those marvellous donors, continued to give to nature during the pandemic. When the appeals they received were passionate, relevant, authentic, personal and moving, they opened their hearts and their wallets.

Bless them.

Made in the USA
Middletown, DE
07 December 2021

54563074R00099